The Wellbeing Zone

Sarah Armitage

Wellbeing is strongly linked to how we see ourselves. In this helpful introduction to the Wellbeing Zone, Armitage shows how the compassion which is key to how we notice, reflect and learn more about ourselves can flow from a deep sense of God's compassion for us. Armitage integrates helpful insights from her own faith and the wisdom of other professionals into what is a comprehensive and accessible model.
I recommend it as a resource to people seeking to learn more about how we flourish as human beings and those looking to bring therapeutic support.

The Very Revd Dr Philip Plyming, Dean of Durham

Within this book Sarah has given a tool for those of us who see in our communities, work and churches people who have been affected by trauma and influences in their past, who we are seeking to help care for and love.

In simple terms, she is able to explain the neurobiology behind responses we see, and how best we can befriend and see healing through our own compassionate responses. Drawing on psychology and spirituality, we are shown how we can enable increased wellbeing in those to whom we minister, and also ourselves. *The Wellbeing Zone* and its understanding is a resource for all who desire to see lives restored, I am grateful for it and hope many will use it as we all learn to live our lives well and flourish.

Sarah Hinton, CEO Shine (West Bowling) Bradford

The Wellbeing Zone by Sarah Armitage blends Christian theology with modern counselling insights to offer a wise and helpful approach to trauma-informed healing and wholeness. The book's PEACE and PRAY models offer practical and compassionate strategies for enhancing our health and resilience. Armitage's approach makes complicated concepts accessible. She encourages us to be curious and compassionate so that we might grow a deeper understanding of ourselves and others. This wonderful book will help us to build a sense of wellbeing that can stand firm in the storms of life, as we use our God-given gifts of reflection and creativity.

Revd Dr David Williams, Director of Training and Development for CMS-Australia

From my standpoint, human wellbeing is a complex, contested and often impenetrable topic. There are so many competing theories with sociologists, theologians, practitioners, psychologists, counsellors, and many others, all weighing in. *The Wellbeing Zone* is, I think, the book that I have been looking for. Sarah offers each of us a timeless guide that is: a) accessible and practical; b) grounded in a balanced, appreciative synthesis of current thinking and c) integrated, recognising that our humanity weaves together physical, emotional, cognitive, relational and spiritual factors. The book is packed with accessible guidance, illustrations and tools.

Together these equip each of us to more confidently and compassionately cultivate our own personal wellbeing as well as the wellbeing of others.

Matthew Frost, independent consultant and coach

Sarah Armitage and I worked together delivering introductory counselling and pastoral care courses over a number of years in Singapore and Cambodia. Sarah is an empathic person with an interest in developing more understanding into effective responses to the psychological impact of trauma. I have been impressed with her extensive research and the Wellbeing Zone in her book, which provides a tool worth pondering for those seeking to help trauma sufferers.

Ron Kallmier, former head of training, CWR UK (now Waverley Abbey Trust)

I have had the privilege of witnessing *The Wellbeing Zone* take shape under Sarah's prayerful dedication to providing an accessible and practical resource that draws from both biblical wisdom and psychological understanding of human flourishing. Based on the Christian understanding that wellbeing is a deep *shalom* that embraces the vicissitudes of living, the early parts of this book read as a companionable mediation on the importance of calibrating our human responses so that we can as far as possible stay within a zone of wellbeing. Crucially this is not a passive place to dwell, but rather a place for moving forward creatively in dynamic and compassionate relationship with ourselves, others and for those with religious faith, our God. With case studies and deep dives into the different areas of the Wellbeing Zone, this book provides rich learning for lay and professional alike.

Kathy Spooner, CEO of Association of Christians in Counselling and Linked Professions (ACC)

Copyright © Sarah Armitage 2024

First published in 2025 by Sarah Grace Publishing
an imprint of Malcolm Down Publishing
www.sarahgracepublishing.co.uk

The right of Sarah Armitage to be identified as the Author of this Work have been asserted by her in accordance with the Copyright, Designs and Patents Act 1988.

All rights reserved. The whole of this work including all text and illustrations is protected by copyright. No part of it may be reproduced, stored in a retrieval system, or transmitted in any form or by any means, electronic, mechanical, photocopying, recording or otherwise, without the prior permission of the publisher or a licence permitting restricted copying – apart from the templates within the appendices, which have been provided for personal use or use with those being seen in a profession or pastoral capacity. In the UK licences are issued by the Copyright Licensing Agency, 5th Floor, Shackleton House, 4 Battle Bridge Lane, London SE1 2HX.

British Library Cataloguing in Publication Data
A catalogue record for this book is available from the British Library.

ISBN: 978-1-917455-33-6

Scripture quotes marked NIVUK are taken from the HOLY BIBLE, NEW INTERNATIONAL VERSION® NIV®. Copyright © 1973, 1978, 1984, 2011 by Biblica, Inc.™ Used by permission of Biblica, Inc.™ All rights reserved worldwide.

Scriptures marked *THE MESSAGE* are taken from *THE MESSAGE*, copyright © 1993, 2002, 2018 by Eugene H. Peterson. Used by permission of NavPress. All rights reserved. Represented by Tyndale House Publishers, Inc.

Scriptures marked Tree of Life are taken from the Tree of Life (TLV) Translation of the Bible. Copyright © 2015 by The Messianic Jewish Family Bible Society.

Cover Design by Esther Kotecha and Daisy Armitage
Art Direction by Sarah Grace

Contents

Preface	11
Acknowledgements	14
Introduction	17
The Wellbeing Zone Table	20

Chapter 1:	Introducing wellbeing	23
Chapter 2:	Introducing the Wellbeing Zone and the PEACE and PRAY models	37
Chapter 3:	Noticing, reflection, curiosity and creativity with compassion	55
Chapter 4:	The Christian beliefs that inform the Wellbeing Zone	71
Chapter 5:	Counselling theories and neuroscience that inform the Wellbeing Zone	87
Chapter 6:	Physical wellbeing	117
Chapter 7:	Emotional wellbeing	131
Chapter 8:	Thinking wellbeing	143
Chapter 9:	Behavioural wellbeing	153
Chapter 10:	Relational wellbeing	163

| Chapter 11: | Spiritual wellbeing | 175 |
| Chapter 12: | Continuing to nurture wellbeing and flourishing | 201 |

References

Appendix A:	The Wellbeing Zone table	209
Appendix B:	The Wellbeing Zone PEACE model and template	215
Appendix C:	The Wellbeing Zone PRAY model and template	219
Appendix D:	The Wellbeing Zone personal plan and team plan templates	223
Appendix E:	The Wellbeing Zone wheel of emotions	227
Appendix F:	The Wellbeing Zone table of common thinking distortions and template for nurturing wellbeing in our thinking life	231
Appendix G:	The Wellbeing Zone template	237

Endnotes 241

Preface

I developed the Wellbeing Zone and the Wellbeing Zone's PEACE and PRAY models to help make trauma-informed counselling theories and interventions accessible and practical. When counselling clients who had experienced fold-or-freeze responses in abusive relationships or traumatic events, I noticed that offering an understanding of the body's neurobiological responses enabled a movement away from feeling overwhelmed, disempowered and confused as to why they had responded in the way they did, towards a compassionate self-understanding. I also noticed feelings of shame and self-blame began to recede. These changes seemed to provide a helpful base from which the features of distress could then be addressed. Alongside this I noticed, too, a greater collaborative quality in the counselling relationship.

As I reflected on these observations, I saw similar themes emerging in my supervision and tutor roles. Non-counselling supervisees whose clients had experienced trauma were asking for skills in helping understand and respond effectively to their client's emotional distress. They were also asking to be equipped in skills for noticing secondary trauma within themselves and the relationships within their organisation. Alongside all this, they wanted to know how best to nurture theirs, their clients' and their colleagues' wellbeing and flourishing. Reflecting on my experience training integrative counsellors, I noticed students were asking how could they discern when to integrate which approach and intervention with their clients.

The Wellbeing Zone and related resources are designed to foster both the cultivation of personal wellbeing as well as the wellbeing of others. I hope this book will be helpful for both counselling professionals as well as anyone who is interested in the topic of nurturing of wellbeing, particularly in the context of trauma and in situations or seasons of life that are specifically demanding, painful or stressful. The Wellbeing Zone resources have been found to be helpful in both pastoral and professional roles where the individuals or communities being served have experiences of adversity or trauma. They are designed to equip the helper and those being helped as, regardless of the role or place we find ourselves in, we share common human survival responses to traumatic or demanding circumstances.

The Wellbeing Zone weaves together Christian theology with counselling and psychological theories. To help illustrate the theories presented and the practical application of the Wellbeing Zone, I have created three fictional characters: Dani, who is in her mid-20s and was entrapped in modern slavery – since being rescued she is receiving supportive care from a Christian charitable organisation; Sam, who is in his mid-50s and heads up a team of support workers for the organisation providing support and care for Dani and for others who have been rescued from modern slavery through trafficking; and Jo, who is in her early 30s and is Dani's support worker. Sam and Jo work in the same organisation.

The Wellbeing Zone table and related resources are created to be used practically. May I encourage you to try out the practical resources as you read? You are welcome to photocopy the blank templates in the appendices for further personal use or use with those you are working with professionally or pastorally.

Acknowledgements

The Wellbeing Zone and the Wellbeing Zone table are the fruit of many generous and deeply valuable conversations I have had the privilege to share with colleagues, friends, family, clients, students and supervisees as I've wrestled with how best to share the helpful understandings and skills within the field of counselling with others: a desire for a 'this is for everyone' stance. I am deeply grateful for each person's insights and wisdom, which are woven into the Wellbeing Zone, and would like to honour their contributions. I would like to highlight my gratitude to the Association of Christians in Counselling and Linked Professions (ACC) for their encouragement and collaboration to expand the Wellbeing Zone's resources following my initial publication of the Wellbeing Zone in their *accord* quarterly journal in the winter of 2022[1] and the subsequent training delivered to counsellors on the Wellbeing Zone through the ACC's training events.

I am deeply grateful to my editor Claire Musters and Kathy Spooner for their editorial wisdom and input. I would also like to say a huge thank you to my niece Daisy, who created the diagram of the brain and the beautiful front cover illustration, and for my son Harry, who kindly created the graphs and charts.

The royalties from this book are being donated to the ACC and to support the development of counselling initiatives in Cambodia. In my former role with CWR/Asia I was involved in the development of a certificate counselling course for pastoral care contexts in Cambodia. The development of counselling initiatives in that country remains dear to my heart.

This book is published in a dyslexia friendly typeface called Grace. Sarah Grace has had the privilege of being the inspiration of the groundbreaking typeface. This unique typeface has been a joint venture with 2K Denmark and Sarah Grace. They worked together for many years to achieve a typeface that eases all kinds of visual stress. Later they collaborated with Cambridge University.

The Grace typeface has proven to be revolutionary due to its defined unique spacing between characters and words, shape of characters, each letter being weighted at the bottom as well as very detailed differences that subtly ease identification of each letter.

I hope this makes your reading experience a more pleasurable one as you journey through this book.

There is also an award winning Bible available in the Grace typeface called the ESV Holy Bible: Dyslexia Friendly Edition published by Crossway.

CSB gospels in the Grace typeface will also be available soon through Malcolm Down and Sarah Grace Publishing.

If you would like more information on the Grace font please do email: sarah@sarahmgrace.co.uk

Introduction

The Wellbeing Zone was created to aid compassionate understanding of the interrelated nature of wellbeing and survival responses. Survival responses are how we instinctively respond to stressful or adverse experiences to enable the best possible survival. Adverse experiences encompass a wide range of life experiences. We have all had days and seasons in life that have been particularly demanding, challenging, painful or difficult. Adverse experiences also include abuse, trauma, the impact of financial or social deprivation, discrimination, oppression, neglect, ill health or abandonment.

Trauma and the consequent search for wellbeing is a huge topic for those of us who have experienced significant trauma and for those seeking to help others impacted by trauma. The effects of trauma can be lifelong and can be intergenerational. Generational trauma is when the psychological and spiritual impacts of adverse events are passed down to future generations.

I want to emphasise right at the outset that the Wellbeing Zone is not a "cure" model. In the search to live well, particularly following distressing traumatic or abusive experiences, the help of specialist practitioners (including medical, counselling, other professionals and groups) may be required to achieve the sense of wellbeing much yearned for. Foundational to any care response is compassionate understanding, which is the bedrock for all counselling and pastoral care initiatives.

As you read you will see I have included some writings from the Bible. The Bible is made up of many books. Where I have quoted from the Bible and given the reference, for example "Luke 1:79", this refers to the book in the Bible called Luke, chapter 1, verse 79.
A verse is made up of one or two sentences that have the same theme.

When you first look at the Wellbeing Zone table you will see that there is a lot of information on one table. This is because we humans are complex beings. It is also because our natural survival responses to adversity and trauma are varied and complex. Likewise, what nurtures our wellbeing is also varied and complex. *The Wellbeing Zone* is designed to be practical – something that can be readily used in everyday life, both in our professional and personal lives. Accordingly, the psychological and counselling theories and Christian theology underpinning the Wellbeing Zone will be explored by focusing on their practical application. If there are topics that you would like to explore in further depth, the reference list provides suggestions for additional reading.

Introduction

We will begin by exploring exactly what wellbeing is in chapter one. We will then look at what the Wellbeing Zone is and how it can be practically applied by using the Wellbeing Zone's PEACE and PRAY models in chapter two. These models were designed to enable noticing, reflection, curiosity and creativity – each with compassion – which research has identified as being foundational practices in fostering wellbeing. Chapter three looks at what these essential qualities are and how they may cultivate wellbeing. Chapter four gives an overview of the Christian beliefs informing the heart of the Wellbeing Zone, and then the underlying psychological and counselling theories are covered in chapter five. The Wellbeing Zone describes six different areas of human life: our physical, emotional, thinking, behavioural, relational and spiritual life. Chapters six to eleven examine each of the six different areas of human life described in the Wellbeing Zone. We will look at how these areas are impacted by stress or trauma, our survival responses and what nurtures wellbeing. Having covered the Wellbeing Zone's informing concepts, the book finishes by looking at how it may be applied in a variety of contexts in our professional and personal lives to help foster wellbeing. In each chapter we will see how the Wellbeing Zone may contribute towards cultivating wellbeing for the characters Dani, Sam and Jo. Their stories serve as illustrations for how the Wellbeing Zone can be helpful for both those in helper roles and for those being helped.

WELLBEING ZONE TABLE

	HYPER-AROUSAL ZONE Fight-or-flight response	**WELLBEING ZONE** Befriending response	**HYPO-AROUSAL ZONE** Freeze-or-fold response
Physical life	Increase in adrenaline; raised heart and breathing rate, blood redirected to muscles, shaking; surge in energy then exhaustion; activation of neurobiological survival responses; increasing vulnerability to stress-related health conditions and diseases; difficulties in sleeping.	Proactive to physical health needs; sense of strength, alertness and energy as health allows.	Exhaustion; lethargy; fatigue; burnout; rundown; neglecting or struggling to be proactive in attending to physical health needs; vulnerable to sickness.
Emotional life	Increasing anxiety, stress, panic, frustration or mis-projected anger. Feeling restless, on-edge, overwhelmed or unsafe; over-reactive; emotional flooding.	Awareness, acceptance and understanding of feelings; being able to respond to emotions that enables wellbeing of self and others; feelings correspond to the situation; compassion; gratitude; hope; empathic to self and others; sense of inner peace.	Feeling low, flat, self-absorbed, depressed, or numb; feelings of shame, disconnection, isolation, helplessness, losing hope; feeling depleted and struggling to be compassionate to self and others; struggling to sense reality and a vulnerability to disconnect from reality.
Thinking life	Becoming focused on past and/or future events; losing perspective; self-absorbed; struggling to think clearly, remember, make decisions or mind going blank or going around in circles; becoming obsessive, judgemental and rigid; catastrophising; narrative may be inconsistent, confusing or incomplete. Distressing memories, intrusive images.	Able to think clearly, objectively and realistically; consider others' perspective and own; thinking is open to new ideas and information; problem solving; able to be reflective; curious and creative; able to give an understandable consistent narrative.	Dwelling on the past and/or future; becoming pulled towards a negative focus, fixed positions, self-absorbed; cynicism; struggling to think clearly, make decisions or going blank; going around in circles; narrative may be inconsistent, confusing, incomplete; vulnerability to dissociate from reality.

Behavioural life	Becoming increasingly obsessive, repetitive, impulsive, hostile, on edge or hyper-vigilant; vulnerable to numbing, spacing-out or addictions.	Attuned to the present moment; responses adapting to the situation to enable the wellbeing and flourishing of self, others and creation; consideration of the past, present and future; courageous; taking initiative; being able to delay gratification; ability to play; creativity.	Becoming passive, withdrawn, isolating and shutdown; drawn towards numbing, spacing out or addictions; operating on autopilot.
Relational life	Becoming increasingly over-reactive, agitated, defensive, avoiding, dominating, demanding, critical, intolerant, exploitative, abusive, self-absorbed or anxious towards others; inclination towards compulsive caretaking or controlling of others; disregarding relational boundaries.	Attunement to and proactive in the development of relationships where all can flourish; sense of relational peace; awareness of and maintenance of healthy relational boundaries; being able to form inter-dependent relationships that are collaborative, accountable and respectful with intimacy and commitment; being humble, tolerant, honest and genuine.	Becoming avoidant, detached, ambivalent, rejecting or dependent in relationships; self-absorbed; vulnerable to others' control, neglect or abuse; losing ability to defend self, initiate responsibility and care of self and others; vulnerability to be unable to maintain healthy boundaries; tendency to be critical of others; struggle to receive affirmation; vulnerability to dissociate from reality.
Spiritual life	Losing the capacity to form and connect with core beliefs, values and sustaining practices that recognise self and others hold infinite worth and care for nature; losing sense of peace, joy and mystery; becoming entitled, impatient and exploitative; struggling to give and receive forgiveness; losing ability to enjoy beauty and sense of awe and wonder; at risk of radicalisation.	Having the capacity to form and connect with core beliefs, values and sustaining practices during suffering and everyday life that recognise self and others hold infinite worth and care of nature; nurturing peace and wellbeing for self and all; giving and receiving forgiveness; accepting mystery; seeking justice for all; holding qualities of hope, compassion, patience, gratitude, generosity and kindness; enjoying beauty and sense of awe and wonder. Altruism.	Losing the capacity to form and connect with core beliefs, values and sustaining practices that recognise self and others hold infinite worth and care for nature; increasing compassion fatigue in care of self, others and creation; becoming bitter; vulnerable to injustice and moral injury; struggling to give and receive forgiveness; sensing emptiness, hopelessness, despair and life is meaningless; struggling to notice and enjoy beauty; losing of sense of awe and wonder.

KEY: Each of us will have a range of unique experiences. We may not experience everything described. This chart is a visual presentation to assist in compassionate awareness and understanding, alongside comprehensive and ongoing assessment. It is not to be used diagnostically or prescriptively. Copyright © Sarah Armitage

Chapter 1

Introducing wellbeing

In this chapter we will look at what wellbeing means and how mental wellbeing may be measured, its link with flourishing and its connection with the concept of *shalom* described in the Bible.

The word "wellbeing" was first introduced into the English language in the 16th century as a translation from the Italian concept of *benessere*, which translates as: "What is good for a person or group?" In the past few decades, the word wellbeing has risen to the fore, initially in health and socio-economic scientific papers where wellbeing is presented as holding specific objective qualities. As a concept, wellbeing has spread to wider culture, but it has been criticised for being ambiguous and subjective; what one person, or group, finds beneficial for living well, another may not.

Within Western Christianity, wellbeing has also become a recent popular concept, giving rise to a plethora of spiritual "wellbeing" resources. The Christian Bible, collated from eyewitness stories and writings nearly two millennia ago (some of the Old Testament is around three millennia old) can be described as a text that offers guidance on what fosters wellbeing, answering the question: "How do we live well?"

Biblical texts were originally written in Hebrew, Aramaic or Koine Greek (the Greek spoken by ordinary people at the time when the New Testament was written). In the Bible, the word *shalom* appears over 250 times in the Old Testament. The Hebrew word *shalom* offers insight into the multi-faceted aspects of wellbeing understood within Christianity. Simply translated, *shalom* means "peace". The New Testament describes the life and teachings of Jesus and the first Christians. The life of Jesus is described as "showing us the way, one foot at a time, down the path of peace" (Luke 1:79, *The Message*).

Shalom can also be translated as "wellbeing". Jesus explained in one of his last teachings to his disciples: "I'm leaving you well and whole. That's my parting gift to you. Peace" (John 14:27, *The Message*). The life of Jesus presents a way of life and relationships where *shalom* is possible:

- for both individuals and communities: "God has called us to make the best of it, as peacefully as we can" (1 Corinthians 7:15, *The Message*)

- for nature: "They took him [Jesus] in the boat . . . A huge storm came up . . . threatening to sink it . . . he told the wind to pipe down and said to the sea 'Quiet! Settle down!' The wind ran out of breath; the sea became smooth as glass" (Mark 4:35–41, *The Message*)

- for a close relationship with God: "We have peace with God through our Lord Jesus" (Romans 5:1, NIVUK).

Within Christianity, God is understood as "above all a compassionate God" (Deuteronomy 4:31, *The Message*). Jesus describes *shalom* as rooted in and flowing from God's compassion: "I've loved you the way my Father has loved me . . . Love one another the way I loved you" (John 15:9,12, *The Message*). To trust in the Christian understanding of a compassionate God, a God that seeks and welcomes humanity into the compassionate relationships within the Trinity – God the Father, Jesus the Son of God and the Holy Spirit – requires faith. Christian faith is understood as trusting in the promises and character of God as revealed in the Bible.

When we think of peace and wellbeing, we may be drawn towards the assumption that all must be well with our lives, that we have everything we need to live well. Being in good health, having adequate finances, living in a comfortable environment, enjoying close warm relationships with others, freedom from stress and adversity are often seen as requirements for wellbeing.

The Warwick-Edinburgh Mental Wellbeing Scales (WEMWBS)[2] were developed to enable the measuring of mental wellbeing when evaluating public policies and programmes. They have been used widely within the UK as well as in other nations. WEMWBS has 14 statements that research has shown are key to psychological wellbeing. Participants are asked to score the following statements:

- I've been feeling optimistic about the future.
- I've been feeling useful.
- I've been feeling relaxed.
- I've been feeling interested in other people.
- I've had energy to spare.
- I've been dealing with problems well.
- I've been thinking clearly.
- I've been feeling good about myself.
- I've been feeling close to other people.
- I've been feeling confident.
- I've been able to make up my own mind about things.
- I've been feeling loved.

- I've been interested in new things.
- I've been feeling cheerful.

High scores in these 14 statements equates with wellbeing. You can see all the statements relate to feelings that would be described as happy or positive feelings.

Jesus, however, taught that *shalom* can be present during suffering: "You will be ... assured, deeply at peace. In this ... world you will continue to experience difficulties" (John 16:33, *The Message*).

In the quest for personal peace and wellbeing, we can be drawn into overlooking others' needs for wellbeing. We have probably all experienced feeling hurt by someone else's behaviour that has overlooked or disregarded our needs for wellbeing. We have probably also, if we are honest, done this to others, especially when we have been tired or under a lot of stress. Our wellbeing then comes at the expense of the needs of others. Our wellbeing can also come at the expense of harming nature. It is generally agreed that the root of the current environmental crisis is humanity overlooking or exploiting creation in the desire to seek short-term wellbeing. Exploitation is the opposite of justice. At the beginning of Jesus' ministry, he announced that his life purpose while living on earth was to preach "good news to the poor ... proclaim freedom for the prisoners and recovery of sight for the blind, to set the oppressed free, to proclaim the year of the Lord's favour" (Luke 4:18–19, NIVUK). The last phrase "to proclaim the year of the Lord's favour" means a resetting in how we live so that all can flourish. Jesus also said he came to "proclaim justice to the nations" (Matthew 12:18, NIVUK). Justice is integral to *shalom.*

The *shalom* Jesus described offers relational pathways in reconciliation: "A new life emerges! . . . this comes from the God who settled the relationship between us and him, and then called us to settle our relationships with each other" (2 Corinthians 5:17–18, *The Message*).

We can see from Jesus' teaching that *shalom* holds both internal and external qualities. Jesus said, "I came so they can have real and eternal life, more and better life than they ever dreamed of'" (John 10:10, *The Message*). In some translations of the Bible this is translated as "they may have life and have it to the full" (including NIVUK). This points towards what is often called "flourishing".

The word "flourishing" was introduced into the English language in the 14th century and is derived from the Anglo-French word *florris*, meaning "to bloom, to grow abundantly, to thrive". Flourishing enables wellbeing and wellbeing enables flourishing. Although different, they are intertwined. Flourishing enables consideration of what external qualities enable wellbeing and thriving. Like wellbeing, these influencing qualities vary for each individual. What environments and factors enable flourishing for one person may be quite different for another. *Shalom* encompasses the many values and qualities that enable humanity and creation to thrive, to grow abundantly, to flourish.

The Wellbeing Zone incorporates the features of *shalom* described in the Bible. However, it refrains from including explicit Christian theology to enable sensitive, ethical application in a broad range of environments.

The Wellbeing Zone was created to bring understanding of:

- self and understanding of how others may be impacted by traumatic events or relationships
- potential normal responses to stressful or traumatic experiences
- common features attributed to wellbeing in our physical, emotional, thinking, behaving, relational and spiritual life
- the interrelated nature of wellbeing and survival responses
- awareness of when the margins of wellbeing may have been reached

- early awareness of compassion fatigue, burnout and secondary trauma for those in "helper" roles

- early awareness of relational or spiritual abuse

- focused interventions that respond to the specific features of an individual's distress

- consideration of how wellbeing may be developed and what enables flourishing for self and others.

The Wellbeing Zone is not to be used prescriptively, but as a tool to invite ongoing compassionate *noticing* of how we or others are experiencing and responding to the challenges of life. It is a tool that assists in individual awareness, alongside fostering awareness of how others are. It can be used, too, when working one-to-one, or in groups.

Jo, Dani and Sam and the Wellbeing Zone

As you read Dani, Sam and Jo's stories, try to notice how external events impacted their ability to flourish.

Jo is a support worker for a Christian charity providing support and care for people who have been rescued from modern slavery. Jo grew up in the same country as Dani, as Jo's parents worked for a charitable organisation teaching medical care in the main regional town. When Jo was 18 years old, she returned to the UK to live and study in London. Initially, she found London unfriendly and unwelcoming and felt overwhelmed with the huge change in lifestyle. There were so many new things to learn: getting around on the Tube and buses, which were the cheapest supermarkets and how to keep safe, as well as adjusting to leaving home and having to do her own laundry and manage her own money. Although Jo had been born in the UK, she had moved abroad with her parents when she was two years old, and so her childhood experience of life in the UK was through annual visits to her grandparents. They lived in a small seaside town where everyone knew them and so were friendly to Jo too.

Jo was aware her teenage years had been very different from her peers; she hadn't had a part-time job and hadn't had the freedom to hang out with friends in the evenings. She'd never been to a music festival and her university peers were talking about musicians she hadn't heard of. She tried to observe what the current fashion styles were but felt she couldn't quite put the right look together. Jo felt very alone. When her peers asked, "Where's your home?", this stirred up feelings of not belonging anywhere, particularly as she knew her parents would be returning to the UK shortly, so she would lose the opportunity to return to her childhood home in the university holidays.

Gradually, over the second year at university, Jo began to find her feet and really enjoy the cultural diversity of living and studying in London. Several of her peers invited her to go along with them to a large church in London that had services and discussion groups focused on enabling students to explore the central beliefs within Christianity and what living life following Jesus' example may look like in the 21st century. Jo found as she read the Gospel stories of Jesus' life that the values he embodied were ones she wanted to live by too. She noticed the experience of listening to others praying in church or in the discussion group cultivated a sense of peace within her, and so she decided that she would commit to living her life following Jesus' example and trusting in the promises of God as described in the Bible. This commitment led to Jo deciding that she would like to work in a role that provided support and care for people who had been rescued from modern slavery after graduating from university. Her church donated finances to this Christian charity, which provided therapeutic care and space for recovery for people of all faiths and none who had been trafficked into the UK for modern slavery.

Dani's country of origin had recently experienced war, shattering their family life and resulting in Dani's family sliding into debt to pay for necessities, including food. When the person whom Dani's family owed money to demanded repayment, the family had no option but to comply with their demand that Dani leave the family home and work for them until the family debts had been repaid. After two months of Dani working long hours doing domestic duties, she was told she would be moved to another country to enable her to repay her family debts quicker. After a long, difficult and frightening journey, Dani was trafficked into the UK and forced into modern slavery. After ten months, Dani was found by the UK police and referred to the charity Sam and Jo work for in order to be given support while the police worked to prosecute her traffickers.

Sam grew up in a deprived neighbourhood in the centre of a large UK city. His early childhood memories include hearing heated family arguments over money. Sam's father left the family home when

Sam was six years old, and since then Sam has had no further contact with his father. Throughout Sam's childhood, his mother worked three low-paid, part-time jobs to provide for her young family. Sam knew his family had little money compared to many of his school friends. Sam's mother has a deep Christian faith. He remembers his mum saying: "God sees us and cares for us all; Father God loves you, me, us all and every living creature very much." Sam also has fond childhood memories of attending services and Sunday lunches at the local community church.

As he looks back on his childhood, Sam is aware of the many sacrifices his mother made to enable him and his siblings to have the best possible childhoods. Sam's mother's Christian spirituality seemed rooted in her knowing and trusting in God's compassion for her, for her family, for others and for nature. She seemed to have a sense of peace in her relationship with God, although she faced huge difficulties bringing up her children as the sole parent with very limited income. Sam's mother, along with Sam's local school, really encouraged education, and he flourished at school as a result. Sam, like his mother, seeks to sincerely live out his Christian faith in adulthood. His Christian faith, along with his childhood experiences, influenced his decision to study sociology at university and his subsequent career as a social worker. He continues to feel a sense of calling to make a positive difference to others. Sam is now a support worker and manager for a Christian charity providing support and care for people who have been rescued from modern slavery.

As part of the charity's ethos to provide trauma-informed support to cultivate their employees' and clients' wellbeing, the staff received training on the Wellbeing Zone. They learned about the core theories within the Wellbeing Zone and how it could be used either one-to-one or in groups to enable holistic understanding of survival responses and the consideration of fostering wellbeing. The staff were shown how the Wellbeing Zone table may aid in discernment of compassion fatigue, burnout or secondary trauma. In this training, time was given for the team to create a wellbeing plan for the staff team, which was recorded using the Wellbeing Zone team plan template (Appendix D). This was regularly reviewed and added to in the monthly team meetings.

The charity uses the WEMWBS to measure the impact of their work. When Dani was initially introduced and her wellbeing assessed, she scored low in all 14 statements. Although Dani was grateful to be placed in temporary housing away from her traffickers, she was frightened for both her and her family's future. While the scale was used with the charity's clients, when Sam personally reflected on the WEMWBS statements, he was aware that he would give himself low scores for: feeling optimistic about the future; feeling relaxed; had energy to spare and feeling cheerful. The cost-of-living crisis in the UK had resulted in Sam's monthly salary no longer allowing him to save each month, so he had recently begun working as a taxi driver at weekends to maintain his family finances. While grateful for the extra work and money, he was aware he was becoming tired and anxious about the future.

Chapter 2

Introducing the Wellbeing Zone and the PEACE and PRAY models

Having looked at wellbeing, flourishing and how they are embedded within the concept of *shalom* described in the Bible, we will now see how these features are woven into the Wellbeing Zone. In chapter two we will discuss the features and purpose of the Wellbeing Zone. Through delving into chapter six of Mark's Gospel we will discover Jesus' response to the traumatic murder of his cousin John the Baptist. The Wellbeing Zone's PEACE and PRAY models are introduced and we will discuss how these models reflect qualities of Jesus' way of being and therefore enable the practical application of the Wellbeing Zone.

The Wellbeing Zone is a holistic table presentation of some of the responses that may be experienced during and following situations or events that are demanding, adverse, stressful, abusive, emotionally or relationally painful, or traumatic. It also gives an overview of a number of features attributed to wellbeing.

The purpose of the Wellbeing Zone is to aid compassionate understanding of the interrelated nature of wellbeing and survival responses. It also brings awareness of when the margins of wellbeing may have been reached. This awareness can similarly assist in the early recognition of burnout and secondary trauma for those in "helper" roles, enabling prompt interventions. Our wellbeing impacts others, and others' wellbeing impacts us. The Wellbeing Zone supports the awareness of our personal wellbeing and also others' wellbeing, including recognition of the patterns of relating that are present in relational or spiritual abuse.

Initially in Western psychology and counselling, the focus was on understanding and easing suffering. Alleviating suffering is different from thriving. To enable thriving requires that we consider what environments and conditions contribute to our flourishing. Our flourishing is dependent on others flourishing and vice versa. The Wellbeing Zone seeks to allow consideration of both alleviating suffering and what contributes to flourishing, for both self and others.

Wellbeing is a dynamic state of being that is constantly changing in response to external and internal influences. The Wellbeing Zone facilitates ongoing noticing of how we and others are experiencing and responding to the challenges of life. This noticing provides the base from which to reflect and be curious in order to discern the focus of helpful actions that nurture wellbeing and flourishing.

Throughout Jesus' life, he displayed the skills of compassionate noticing, reflection and curiosity. At any given moment, Jesus was aware of what was going on in the world around him and within himself. His noticing, reflection and curiosity led to him compassionately create new ways to live that fostered wellbeing and flourishing, which we are invited to live too. An example of this is found in the Gospel of Mark.

Chapter 6 in Mark's Gospel contains two dramatic stories that have become embedded within Western cultural narratives: the "Beheading of John the Baptist" – the gruesome story of one of the world's despotic leaders misusing their position of power to control and abuse others, including murdering John the Baptist – and then the "Feeding of the 5,000", the story of trying to meet overwhelming, desperate needs with totally inadequate resources and how Jesus miraculously fed 5,000 people with five loaves and two fish. Sandwiched between these two striking stories is a simple six-sentence story that is easy to overlook:

> The apostles gathered round Jesus and reported to him all they had done and taught. Then, because so many people were coming and going that they did not even have a chance to eat, he said to them, "Come with me by yourselves to a quiet place and get some rest." So they went away by themselves in a boat to a solitary place. But many who saw them leaving recognised them and ran on foot from all the towns and got there ahead of them. When Jesus landed and saw a large crowd, he had compassion on them, because they were like sheep without a shepherd. So he began teaching them many things.
>
> *(Mark 6:30-34, NIVUK)*

This short, unassuming account provides insight into how Jesus responded to profoundly distressing, traumatic events. The story captures Jesus' noticing of his and others' physical, emotional, thinking, behavioural, relational and spiritual life. John the Baptist was Jesus' cousin, so his death was a deeply personal traumatic bereavement. But it also ignited the dramatic societal, religious and political ramifications of a high-profile grotesque murder. The context within which John the Baptist was murdered was one of abuse, exploitation, a disregard for ethical values and a desire for power and revenge. Jesus' response at the "Feeding of the 5,000" is a counterpoint, showing a way of living in the midst of distressing events that nurtures the wellbeing and flourishing of all, a way of living where all are welcome, where needs are understood and compassionately met through the sharing of resources.

Jesus also revealed the importance of recognising when we and others around us need to take time for rest and renewal, especially when caring for or serving others. In this way he showed that compassion is kindness, comprised of compassionate noticing, reflection, curiosity and creativity. Jesus shared his time of rest with his disciples; in doing this, Jesus shows us the importance of taking time to:

- attend to our own spirituality
- notice and be in nature
- be with friends with whom we can mutually receive and talk through what is on our hearts and how we have been impacted by events
- be restored and have the capacity to respond to the needs of the world around us.

We have already seen that the life of Jesus is described as "showing us the way, one foot at a time, down the path of peace" (Luke 1:79, *The Message*). The Wellbeing Zone's PEACE and PRAY models offer a practical structure in which to consider how we too may live that path of peace.

Jesus' life was one of constant prayer with God. For Jesus, prayer included taking time to notice how he was experiencing life in a given moment, notice his thoughts and feelings, notice what was happening around him, notice the compassionate presence of God and discern what God was inviting him to do. Jesus provided us with a model of how to pray in what is called "The Lord's Prayer" (Matthew 6:9-13; Luke 11:2-4). The Lord's Prayer offers a pattern of responding (in prayer) to the nurturing of wellbeing relationships with ourselves, with others, with creation and with God. The Wellbeing Zone's PEACE and PRAY models offer a practical structure in which to consider how we may also live that life of prayer.

The PEACE and PRAY models explained

The Wellbeing Zone's PEACE and PRAY models provide a structure to invite sensitivity and creativity about responding to specific features of distress, so that wellbeing and flourishing may be nurtured. They were created to be used alongside the Wellbeing Zone table and offer an easy-to-remember, practical method to apply the compassionate skills of noticing, reflection, curiosity and creativity when using the Wellbeing Zone.

The mnemonic PEACE stands for **Pause, Enquire, Ask, Create** and **Engage**.

I have found some Christians prefer the mnemonic PRAY as they already have an established pattern of praying and so find it easier to include the Wellbeing Zone's PRAY model into their daily habits of prayer and attending to their wellbeing. The mnemonic PRAY has been used by many authors to create helpful structures to support the development of a Christian prayer life.[3]

The mnemonic PRAY stands for **Pause, Reflect, Ask** and **Yield**. Prayer usually brings to mind a spiritual practice. For Christians, prayer is central to living life. However, 'pray' can also mean to hope or wish for wellbeing and therefore is accessible to anyone wanting to adopt the PRAY model, whether Christian or otherwise.

The PEACE and PRAY models include the same practical skills to enable the application of the Wellbeing Zone. I have found for those who do not hold a pattern of praying in their everyday life, the PEACE model is more helpful, as people connect to the value of bringing peace to both themselves and to others. Use whichever model you sense would work best for you when you are personally using the Wellbeing Zone. When you are using the Wellbeing Zone in a pastoral or professional role, consider what would be the most appropriate model for the people and context in which you are working.

How to begin using the PEACE and PRAY models

The Wellbeing Zone table has a lot of information within one page and can feel a bit daunting when first looking at it. I have found the more someone incorporates the Wellbeing Zone table and PEACE or PRAY models into their reflective practices, whether this is in their spiritual practices, in their work with a professional counsellor, pastoral or support worker or in supervision for counselling or another role, the more familiar they become with it and they begin to instinctively use it in both their professional roles and everyday life. This enables the ability to notice when we are moving out of the wellbeing zone for an aspect of life and then respond to nurture our wellbeing.

Like learning any new skill, the ability to respond with compassion takes time and effort to learn, as do the skills of noticing, reflection, curiosity and creativity. This can be hard when we are in the hypo-arousal or hyper-arousal zones, that is when we are feeling very tired or in a low mood, or are feeling quite anxious or angry. When we are in these zones (and also when we are in the wellbeing zone) it is key that we are compassionate to ourselves. Ask yourself the question, "Am I being compassionate to myself?" You may notice that your thinking includes judgemental, negative or anxious focused thoughts about yourself or the situation. Instead of responding to these distressing thoughts, choose to be compassionate to yourself. You might like to consider saying to yourself, "I want to grow in being compassionate to myself. I recognise this is a new thing for me and will take time and effort to learn. However, I choose now to be compassionate to myself, to be kind to myself" and then follow the PEACE or PRAY model to consider how you might be compassionate to yourself right now. This may include being patient with yourself, making choices that nurture your wellbeing.

It is helpful to not have distractions when you are first learning to engage with the PEACE or PRAY model. Find a place where you can be peaceful and uninterrupted to look at the Wellbeing Zone table and then follow the instructions on either the PEACE or PRAY models. The benefits of being able to notice and calibrate experiences, both in our professional and personal lives, are that we can stay more in the wellbeing zone and from that zone be more likely to make decisions that nurture our wellbeing for ourselves and for others.

When using the PEACE or PRAY model, you might find it helpful to have a copy of the Wellbeing Zone table and template and a journal or the PEACE or PRAY templates at hand to note down your initial observations, reflections and questions (see appendices B and C). This can be helpful to refer to as well as notice any changes. At first, the skill of noticing can be difficult, but the more you practise, the more you will improve and become able to use the skills in everyday life. You may find it helpful to go through the PEACE or PRAY model with someone to begin with. Take time to *reflect* on what you've *noticed* and then move on to the *curiosity* and *creativity* steps. You are welcome to print copies of these for further personal use or use with those you are working with professionally or pastorally.

Wellbeing Zone PEACE model

Pause	Take a few steady breaths, breathing in through your nose for the count of four, holding your breath for the count of four, then breathing out through your nose for the count of four, resting for the count of four and then repeating the cycle several times. Now take time to notice your physical body. How do the different parts of your body feel? You may like to begin at your toes and move up through your body to your head, noticing any signs of tension, discomfort or ease. Reflect on your energy levels, overall health, daily sleep, rest, diet and exercise patterns. Then move your noticing to your emotional, thinking, behavioural, relational and spiritual life. Ask yourself these questions: What feelings do I notice? We often can feel a mixture of feelings at the same time. What do I notice about the thoughts I am having now? Are these thoughts generally hopeful and do they nurture wellbeing and flourishing, or are they distressing? Is there a pattern to my thoughts and if so, what might this pattern be? What patterns of behaviour am I drawn towards? What do I notice about how I am relating to others? What do I notice about my spiritual life? What do I notice about how my feelings, thoughts, behaviours, ways of relating and my spiritual life impact on one another?
Enquire	How would I describe what I notice? How does this relate to the descriptions in the Wellbeing Zone? Which zones (hyper-arousal, hypo-arousal or wellbeing) do I sense I am in for each of the areas of my life?
Ask	What do I and others desire or need to help nurture wellbeing and flourishing?
Create	What resources can I draw on? What new skills or changes would be helpful to develop? How could I do this? When could I start to do this?
Engage	What compassionate choice(s) can I make to nurture wellbeing and flourishing? How do my choices nurture others and their wellbeing and flourishing? How do my choices care for nature?

The Wellbeing Zone PRAY model

Pause	Take a few steady breaths, breathing in through your nose for the count of four, holding this breath for the count of four, then breathing out through your nose for the count of four, resting for the count of four and then repeating the cycle several times. Now take time to notice your physical body. How do the different parts of your body feel? You may like to begin at your toes and move up through your body to your head, noticing any signs of tension, discomfort or ease. Reflect on your energy levels, overall health, daily sleep, rest, diet and exercise patterns.
	Then move your noticing to your emotional, thinking, behavioural, relational, and spiritual life. Ask yourself these questions:
	What feelings do I notice? We often can feel a mixture of feelings at the same time.
	What do I notice about the thoughts I am having now? Are these thoughts generally hopeful and do they nurture wellbeing and flourishing, or are they distressing? Is there a pattern to my thoughts and if so, what might this pattern be?
	What patterns of behaviour am I drawn towards?
	What do I notice about how I am relating to others?
	What do I notice about my spiritual life?
	What do I notice about how my feelings, thoughts, behaviours, ways of relating and my spiritual life impact on one another?
Reflect	How would I describe what I notice?
	How does this relate to the descriptions in the Wellbeing Zone?
	Which zones (hyper-arousal, hypo-arousal or wellbeing) do I sense I am in for each of the areas of my life?
Ask	What do I and others desire or need to help nurture wellbeing and flourishing?
	What resources can I draw on?
	What new skills or changes would be helpful to develop?
	How could I do this?
	When could I start to do this?
Yield	What compassionate choice(s) can I make to nurture wellbeing and flourishing?
	How do my choices nurture others and their wellbeing and flourishing?
	How do my choices care for nature?

Considerations when using the Wellbeing Zone and PEACE and PRAY models with others

In professional or pastoral contexts, when working through the PEACE and PRAY models with another person, it's important that these models are not imposed or prescribed. Rather, they are tools to be explored gently and by invitation. Similarly, when referring to the Wellbeing Zone table, the simple descriptions offered may or may not match those chosen by a person as they are describing what they are noticing or experiencing. It is important to use the words and descriptions that come naturally to the person.

A note for professional counsellors: although the PEACE and PRAY models and Wellbeing Zone lend themselves well to professional counselling practice and have clear assessment qualities, this approach is not being proposed as an alternative to an initial or ongoing clinical assessment.

The PEACE and PRAY models and the Wellbeing Zone table have value also in offering a way to enhance collaboration and mutual understating within professional working relationships, especially within a therapeutic context, for example in counselling, pastoral or cross-professional supervision.

Jo, Dani and Sam and the PEACE model

Sam and Jo have been providing support to Dani over the past two months. Jo speaks Dani's language as she grew up in Dani's country. Initially Dani was naturally very wary of Sam and Jo. However, gradually she has begun to share details of her past life, journey to the UK and how she is experiencing life now. The charity has a comprehensive assessment form for each person that is recorded on an ongoing basis as more information is understood about each person, either from the person or from other support professionals. Jo and Sam have noticed Dani often appears tired, anxious and distressed.

As part of the support offered to Dani, she attends a weekly wellbeing group for women who have experienced modern slavery, which seeks to empower the women with skills to foster their wellbeing. Jo has translated the Wellbeing Zone table into Dani's language. In today's group they are looking at the skill of noticing and the Wellbeing Zone's PEACE model. Using the PEACE model template, Dani writes down what she notices within herself on the "Pause" and "Enquire" sections.

As Dani follows Jo's guidance on taking a few steady breaths and then noticing how her body feels, she is aware of her tummy feeling tight. Jo invites Dani and the others in the group to notice their levels of energy and overall health. Jo then explains how our diet and daily sleep, rest and exercise patterns play an essential part in fostering our wellbeing. Since the war broke out, Dani has found it difficult to fall to sleep, and experienced restless nights after being taken from her family. She has felt tired constantly and had a series of lingering chest infections. Apart from attending appointments with her support workers, Dani remains inside her temporary housing room so does little exercise and struggles to eat regular meals (she has lost her appetite since being taken from her home and Dani finds the UK local supermarkets are very different from the markets back home).

As Dani reads the Wellbeing Zone table, she can identify with many of the descriptions in the red hyper-arousal and blue hypo-arousal zones. Dani writes down her observations in the Wellbeing Zone's PEACE model template. Jo's compassionate, respectful, curious questions enable Dani to reflect further and expand her noticing. Dani finds Jo's simple description of the body's neurological survival responses helpful in understanding herself and her reactions since the outbreak of the war. Jo explains to Dani that when we encounter situations that are demanding, adverse, stressful, abusive or traumatic, hyper-arousal responses are our body's first-line survival responses (these are described in the red section of the Wellbeing Zone table). Jo goes on to explain that hyper-arousal responses cannot be maintained forever and that eventually the body will exhaust its resources, and we then move into hypo-arousal responses to enable the body to rest and restore (these are in the blue section of the Wellbeing Zone table). Looking at the table, Dani begins to recognise how her body has adapted to help her survive an immensely traumatic time. Dani can see the reason behind the changes within herself and this understanding enables Dani to be compassionate to herself instead of feeling confused and frightened as to why she has experienced so many distressing changes within herself since leaving her family home. Jo also explains to the group that when we have been in relationships or situations where we have been denied choices, it can take a while to fully consider what we may need or desire to nurture our wellbeing and flourishing. Jo also explains that over the next few weeks the group will take time to consider the "Ask, Create and Engage" sections of the Wellbeing Zone's PEACE model, and emphasises the importance of being patient and kind to ourselves, as it takes a while to learn new skills.

The charity provides monthly psychological supervision by experienced counselling supervisors for all their support workers, to enable their staff to reflect on their work and how it impacts them personally. Sam received one-to-one supervision and the rest of his team, including Jo, had group supervision with a different supervisor to enable a safe, confidential space. Before supervision, Sam used the Wellbeing Zone's PEACE model to reflect on his wellbeing over the past month, both professionally and personally. It had been a difficult month as the charity's funding was being frozen, alongside several clients reporting they were regularly skipping meals due to a lack of money. As he reflected after taking several steady breaths in through his nose for the count of four, holding his breath for the count of four, then breathing out through his nose for the count of four, resting for the count of four and then repeating the cycle several times, he became aware his thinking had become preoccupied with anxiety concerning his family finances. Sam was also aware the freezing of funding evoked feelings of frustration and anxiety about the level of services the organisation would be able to provide in the future. Sam recorded what he had noticed across the physical, emotional, thinking, behavioural, relational and spiritual areas of his life on a copy of the Wellbeing Zone's PEACE model personal plan template and shared his observations with his supervisor. Reflecting on his observations with his supervisor, Sam became aware that the charity's financial situation was beginning to impact his thought life the most, with his mind preoccupied with trying to figure out how to respond to the financial difficulties.

We will look at Jo, Dani and Sam's observations in more detail in the following chapters.

Chapter 3

Noticing, reflection, curiosity and creativity with compassion

We have seen in chapter two that noticing, reflection, curiosity and creativity with compassion shaped Jesus' response to the traumatic murder of John the Baptist. In chapter three we will look at these qualities in more depth from a Christian perspective and see that they are linked to current counselling research in facilitating wellbeing. When looking at the skill and practice of reflection, we will see how a widely used tool called the Johari Window highlights the value of growing in self-awareness.

Daniel Siegal is a world-leading intrapersonal neurobiologist whose research identified that the skills of noticing, reflection, curiosity and creativity with compassion are foundational for nurturing personal and community wellbeing and flourishing.[4] These skills enable the development of awareness and understanding of ourselves, of others and our relationships with others as well as the world we live in. This provides a useful starting point to consider what may be helpful in cultivating personal wellbeing, alongside the wellbeing and flourishing of others and the environment. For those wondering what 'intrapersonal neurobiology' is, it is the study of how human relationships are shaped by our bodies' biological responses to previous experiences of relationships. Intrapersonal neurobiology gives us understanding of how our past may impact our response to a current situation and how the six areas of life within the Wellbeing Zone interconnect.

Daniel Siegal explains that awareness has three parts: focused attention, open awareness and kind intention.[5]

- **Focused attention** is choosing to keep our mind focused on something and returning to that focus when we become distracted.
- **Open awareness** is the choice to be 'open' or curious about what we may notice.
- **Kind intention** is another way of saying compassion.

Awareness provides the foundation to nurture emotional balance. Emotional balance increases the quality of relational presence a person brings to others by a sense of calmness, composure and compassion. Awareness also provides the foundation to respond well to life's challenges. It provides the base for interventions to be targeted on the features of the distress or difficulties present. When we experience severe distress, we can be unaware that we are getting drawn into either rigid or chaotic responses, instead of helpful adaptive ones.

Compassion

Compassion is understood within Christianity as rooted in the belief that each person is created in the "image of God" and therefore holds infinite worth (Genesis 1:27, NIVUK). No matter what a person may have done or who they are, each person has infinite worth. Compassion is the choice to be kind to ourselves, to others and, by extension, to creation. Compassion begins by choosing to connect with how we, others and nature may be experiencing life in each moment, including seeking to understand any external and internal influences.

A note on empathy

Empathy is the ability to understand the feelings of another person and is a fundamental quality in caring relationships. Research into empathy has identified that there are different types of empathy.[6,7]

- **Emotional empathy** is when you literally feel what another person is feeling. This can lead to a vulnerability of taking on others' emotions. We can lose objectivity and become at risk of compassion fatigue and burnout.

- **Cognitive empathy** is empathy of thought; seeing another person's perspective, while refraining from engagement with their emotions. While cognitive empathy can be helpful in professional and other roles that require complex thinking to enable the welfare of another person, that person may be left feeling we don't fully care about them.

- **Compassionate empathy** is the ability to understand both the feelings and thoughts of another person, take action to help them as well as being considerate to our own feelings, thoughts and wellbeing. When asked about how to live well, Jesus emphasised that we are each to "love your neighbour as yourself" (Matthew 19:19, Mark 12:31, Luke 10:27, NIVUK).

Christians believe that when Jesus was living on earth, he was both fully God and fully human. In this duality, Jesus was the embodiment of compassionate empathy because he could fully understand what it was to be human, and in his teachings and ultimately his suffering and death, he was acting out of divine compassion for humanity. During Jesus' earthly life, his compassion for others often led him out of his human comfort zone. An example of this is when Jesus was wrestling with anguish in the Garden of Gethsemane as he knew what suffering lay before him with his crucifixion and death (Matthew 26:36-46; Mark 14:32-42; Luke 22:39-46). The suffering and death of Jesus is the ultimate example for Christians that acting compassionately can mean that sometimes we need to move out of our comfort zones and experience loss and suffering. Jesus calls his followers, too, to move out of comfortable environments to care for others (Matthew 28:19).

The first step to connecting with ourselves, with others and with creation is the act of observing with compassionate empathy. That is seeking to understand and accept our thoughts and feelings, and also how others involved in the situation are impacted, without judgement. When we notice, if we become aware of uncomfortable or distressing feelings or thoughts (for example feelings of shame or anger), we can refrain from judging or seeking to avoid or deny these difficult thoughts and feelings and instead consider what these thoughts and feelings show us about how we or others have been impacted by a situation. Then, using the PEACE or PRAY model, we can consider how we may respond with compassionate empathy and kind intention to nurture wellbeing and flourishing for both ourselves and others.

Compassionate noticing

Compassionate noticing is taking time to become aware of what is happening in our physical body, as well as in our emotional, thinking, behavioural, relational and spiritual life, with loving understanding and kindness towards ourselves rather than judging, being critical or avoiding what we notice.

Other words for noticing include: attention, awareness, mindfulness, seeing, recognising, noting, observing, spotting.

Noticing requires that we are present or fully engaged with ourselves and with others – that we intentionally seek to live in the present moment. Within Christianity, prayer can be understood as being present in the presence of God in loving awareness. The Lord's Prayer includes the line "Give us each day our daily bread" (Luke 11:3, NIVUK), which means asking God for our daily needs for wellbeing.

Noticing provides the foundation to then consider the question: "What will nurture wellbeing?" In the parable of the Prodigal Son (Luke 15:11-32), a story about God's loving care for humanity, it was when the son "came to his senses" (Luke 15:17, NIVUK) that he was able to make choices that enabled his wellbeing. Another, different, example is described in Luke in the time after Jesus' death, when his disciples felt utterly confused, overwhelmed with grief and lacking in hope. Following Jesus' resurrection, he repeated the actions from his last supper with the disciples before his crucifixion by giving thanks and breaking bread and "their eyes were opened... they recognised him [Jesus]" (Luke 24:31, NIVUK). This "recognising" enabled the disciples to then take actions that rekindled their hope and life purpose.

Two American psychologists, Joseph Luft and Harrington Ingham, developed the "Johari Window",[8] a simple quadrant drawing that shows how awareness can assist in gaining understanding. Interestingly, "Johari" is Arabic for "jewel", signifying how precious awareness is.

The Johari Window

	Known to self	Not known to self
Known to others	**Open self** Information about you that you and others know	**Blind spot** Information about you that you don't know but others do know
Not known to others	**Hidden self** Information about you that you know but others don't know	**Unknown self** Information about you that you and others don't know

The open self can be expanded through growing in personal awareness. The hidden self can be reduced by sharing information about yourself with others. The blind spot can be reduced through inviting feedback from others.

As the open self grows, so our blind spot, hidden self and unknown self diminish. Self-understanding reflective practices, for example inviting feedback from others, taking time to notice, reflect and be curious about ourselves, about others, and about our world, enable details that we were initially unaware of to come into our conscious recognition. Christians believe that prayer can also bring to light things we were previously unaware of. There are many different types of prayers within Christian spiritualty, for example prayers of giving thanks to God, adoration for who God is, confessing when we have hurt others or done something we regret and asking God to intervene in a situation. Prayer can also include our conversations with God as we wrestle with questions. The Old Testament prophet Job, who experienced a profound season of suffering, describes how God "reveals the deep things of darkness and brings utter darkness into the light" (Job 12:22, NIVUK).

To grow in the skill of compassionate noticing, try putting into words what draws your attention in the present moment, around you and within you. Allow time to notice and name the details of what you observe. You may want to use the PEACE or

PRAY model personal plan template to write down what you notice.

Compassionate reflection

Reflection draws our attention to the present moment. It is allowing time to carefully consider what we notice, and then begin to consider what may be influencing ours' and others' wellbeing. Our ability to reflect lies at the heart of emotional, relational and social intelligence. Making time for reflection can be hard if we have many demands upon us and our lives are busy.

Compassionate reflection enables us to:

- learn more about ourselves (self-awareness), about others and about creation, including what has helped shape and influenced these

- learn from experience

- bring things out into the open, enabling a fuller understanding and allowing the truth to be uncovered

- allow reactions and patterns to be noticed in ourselves, in others and in nature – in our physical, emotional, thinking, behavioural, relational and spiritual life

- allow experiences to be framed (put into context), and maybe reframed (thinking about them differently, especially from another perspective)

- allow searching questions to be considered, including questioning our values, beliefs, meanings, assumptions, prejudices, habitual patterns and our understanding

- grow in our spirituality – Christian reflective practices can provide the space to explore our relationship with God

- allow creativity – a fresh perspective, to "think outside the box", to come up with a new idea

- increase our emotional balance and compassionate relational presence.

Compassionate reflection provides the foundation for wisdom, maturity and development. Instead of being drawn into automatic, immediate responses (often called "acting self" in counselling terminology), the ability to notice, observe and then make informed choices increases our capacity to bring *shalom* to our environments (often called "observing self" in counselling terminology).

Compassionate curiosity

Compassionate curiosity is taking time to think through what questions may be helpful to enable greater understanding of what we have discovered in our reflections on self, others, creation and spirituality, questions like: Why? What? How? When? Where? Which? Who? Would? Ask these questions with compassionate empathy, seeking kind intention, rather than from a critical, shaming, prideful or angry position.

The Gospel stories show Jesus asking questions that encouraged the other person to be curious and to widen and deepen their breadth of understanding about themselves, others, the world and God. An example of this is in the Gospel of Mark (8:27-29) when Jesus asked the disciples, "Who do people say I am?" (NIVUK). Jesus was inviting the disciples to reflect on and be curious about what they had experienced since knowing him, and how this may have linked to their understanding of the Jewish texts. The disciples responded with, "Some say John the Baptist; others say Elijah; and still others, one of the prophets." Jesus encouraged the disciples to think deeper about the question by asking, "But what about you?... Who do you say I am?" Peter then answered with: "You are the Messiah." Jesus' questions fostered the disciples' curiosity and they were able to deepen their understanding of who he is.

The Gospel stories also show how someone's curiosity about who Jesus is can lead to transformative change for the person. An example is in the Gospel of Luke (19:1-10). Zacchaeus was a chief collector of taxes and the story reveals that he was corrupt. He charged higher taxes and kept the difference. Zacchaeus' encounter with Jesus led to Zacchaeus choosing to publicly confess his dishonesty and offer to pay back four times the amount of money he had taken from others.

Compassionate curiosity is foundational for discovering new knowledge and for considering what may be the best choices for nurturing wellbeing and flourishing.

Compassionate creativity

Creativity is the courage to change and create, discover, learn and try out new ways of responding to situations that nurture our and others' wellbeing. Seeking to live life following Jesus' example requires the courage to trust in God's compassion. The early followers of Jesus were invited to "live creatively, friends" (Galatians 6:1, *The Message*). Compassionate creativity can be nurtured through questions like: "I wonder if . . . ?", "What might be different if . . . ?", "How can we . . . ?", "What would it be like to . . . ?". Compassionate creativity refrains from judging questions as either wrong or stupid and instead seeks to widen the perspective to explore potential possibilities from different outlooks. In the Gospel story about Zacchaeus, he climbed a tree to get a better view of Jesus (Luke 19:3-4). Zacchaeus was creative.

Consider what fosters your creativity. Are there places, people or activities that nurture your creativity? Be compassionate to yourself when trying out new ways of responding to situations. Instead of expecting instant success or mastery of a new skill, be compassionate to yourself by being curious. It takes courage to do something you haven't done before and new skills take time to fully develop. The questions: "What have I learned from what I tried?" and "What might I do differently next time?" can further cultivate compassionate creativity.

Sam and noticing, reflection, curiosity and creativity with compassion

Sam's days were full of activity at work and at home. He valued the time and space that his monthly supervision gave him, alongside his daily pattern of reflecting and praying on his walk to and from work. These times allowed him space to focus his attention and be more openly aware about what he noticed in a given moment compared to the busyness at home and work. Sam found the structure offered through the Wellbeing Zone's PEACE model a helpful tool to guide his reflective practice – personally, with his supervisor and with conversations with colleagues.

When his supervisor enquired about what may be contributing to his thinking being preoccupied with finances, Sam noticed a couple of distant memories of his parents arguing popping into his mind, along with the thought, "I don't want my family life to break down like my dad's relationship with my childhood family." He was surprised by how anxious he suddenly felt, noticing a tightness across his chest. As Sam considered this thought further, he could see the link between his childhood experiences of family relationships and his current situation which he'd previously been blind to. His immediate reaction was to tell himself, "Don't be so silly," that he was catastrophising and being too emotional. His supervisor enquired if he had noticed other times over the past month when he had become more emotional than normal. As Sam reflected over his conversations with clients, he became aware that when the topic was on not having enough money and skipping meals, he had begun to take on his client's emotional reactions, which then seemed to trigger his catastrophising thinking.

Sam also shared his concerns about the organisation's funding being frozen. His supervisor's question of, "How would you like to be able to respond?" enabled Sam to then consider how he could regain his sense of emotional balance at both work and home. Instead of feeling pressurised to immediately respond to the challenges around him, Sam committed to try to take a minute to pause, notice what was happening both within himself and in the other person, and then consider what would be the best response to the situation.

His curiosity led Sam to think through how he intended to be kind to himself by replacing the phrase "Don't be so silly" with "It's understandable why someone with my background may have these immediate thoughts and feelings." Sam also decided that being compassionate to himself included taking time to discuss the family finances with his spouse, as he was aware he had leaped into working weekends without really talking through the family's financial situation first. He also wondered if it would be good to review the charity's resources and support to clients who were experiencing financial difficulties, especially in relation to accessing adequate food.

His supervisor invited Sam to explore how the freezing of funding had presented a moral injury for him. The funding allocation had been decided by an external organisation to the charity he worked for, yet Sam held the responsibility for deciding the cuts to the service. He also saw first-hand the impact of the cuts, which challenged his deeply held value that people who are in difficult circumstances through no fault of their own should be given care and support. By his supervisor inviting him to reflect on his personal ethical values and his emotional responses in relation to the funding freezing, Sam saw the link between his feelings and his value of justice and supportive care for others because of his belief that each person has infinite worth.

At the end of the supervision session, Sam felt a renewed sense of compassionate empathy in his professional and personal relationships. He was aware that his emotional empathic responses over the past month were contributing to him feeling exhausted, as was working weekends. Sam was grateful for the creativity of the structured session, a time to pause, enquire, ask, create and then engage with the current challenges.

Chapter 4

Christian beliefs that inform the Wellbeing Zone

Having explored wellbeing and how the Wellbeing Zone can assist in the thoughtful consideration of nurturing wellbeing, chapter four will look at the Christian theology that informs the Wellbeing Zone. In it we will look at the Christian belief that humanity is made in the image of God and how this has shaped the features of the Wellbeing Zone. The Wellbeing Zone includes consideration of spirituality. We will also look at how the Bible offers narratives and wisdom when seeking to respond well to adverse experiences, including trauma.

Humanity is made in the image of God

Embedded in the Wellbeing Zone is the Christian belief that humanity is made in the image of God. In the first book of the Bible, Genesis, humanity is described by God as being made "in our image"

(Genesis 1:27, *The Message*). This informs the Christian belief that each person has innate, infinite worth, that each person is uniquely important and that their life is profoundly precious. The first three chapters of Genesis describe how humanity is innately created for *shalom*, or 'wellbeing' relationships with self, with others, with nature and with God. Being made in the image of God means we have a physical, emotional, thinking, behaving, relating and spiritual life as the Bible describes God holding these characteristics.

- **Physical life:** When Jesus was living on earth, he had a physical human body like me and you (John 1:14). Jesus was born from his mother Mary (Luke 2:6-7) and grew up to be man doing the physical things humans do. The Gospels describe Jesus eating, drinking, sleeping and walking (see for example Mark 4:38 and John 4:6-7). God is described in the Old Testament as having human physical features. For example, "The Lord would speak to Moses face to face, as one speaks to a friend" (Exodus 33:11, NIVUK); "The eyes of the Lord are everywhere, keeping watch on the wicked and the good" (Proverbs 15:3, NIVUK).

- **Emotional life:** The Gospels describe Jesus experiencing and expressing many deep emotions while he lived on earth. Examples include: "He looked around at them in anger and, deeply distressed at their stubborn hearts" (Mark 3:5, NIVUK); "When Jesus landed and saw a large crowd, he had compassion on them, because they were like sheep without a shepherd" (Mark 6:34, NIVUK); "I have told you this so that my joy may be in you and that your joy may be complete" (John 15:11, NIVUK); "As the Father has loved me, so have I loved you" (John 15:9, NIVUK). God the Father is described expressing a wide range of emotions: "a compassionate and gracious God, slow to anger, abounding in love and faithfulness" (Psalm 86:15, NIVUK).

- **Thinking life:** Isaiah 55:8-9 describes God having a thinking life: "'For my thoughts are not your thoughts, neither are your ways my ways' declares the Lord. 'As the heavens are higher than the earth, so are my ways higher than your ways and my thoughts than your thoughts'" (NIVUK).

- **Behavioural life:** In the verses above (Isaiah 55:8-9) we see God's behaviour described as "ways". The Gospels are full of descriptions of Jesus' behaviour when he lived on earth. For example, when Jesus was 12 years old, his parents "found him in the temple courts, sitting among the teachers, listening to them and asking them questions" (Luke 2:46, NIVUK).

- **Relational life:** The Bible describes the relational life of God within each person of God (the Trinity) and between each different person of God: "I and the Father are one" (John 10:30, NIVUK) and "As soon as Jesus was baptised, he went up out of the water. At that moment heaven was opened, and he saw the Spirit of God descending like a dove and alighting on him. And a voice from heaven said, 'This is my Son, whom I love; with him I am well pleased" (Matthew 3:16-17, NIVUK). It also describes the relationship between God and humanity: "My dwelling-place will be with them: I will be their God, and they will be my people" (Ezekiel 37:27, NIVUK), "The one who loves me will be loved by my Father, and I too will love them and show myself to them" (John 14:21, NIVUK).

- **Spiritual life:** When Jesus lived on earth, as we've seen in the passages above, he had a spiritual life: he went to the temple courts (Luke 2:46); he was baptised (Matthew 3:16-17); he understood scripture, as over a tenth of Jesus' spoken words recorded in the gospels refer to texts in the Old Testament; he regularly took time to pray with his Father (God) (Luke 5:16). We've also already seen Jesus' life purpose was "showing us the way, one foot at a time, down the path of peace" (Luke 1:79, *The Message*).

Christian beliefs that inform the Wellbeing Zone

These innate features of human life are delineated on the Wellbeing Zone table and show how we can oscillate between different zones at any given time. For example, at the end of a particularly difficult and demanding week, our physical, thinking and behavioural life may be in the hypo-arousal zone. We may be feeling physically exhausted, our thoughts full of all that has gone wrong, and we may feel on autopilot as we take a meal out of the freezer to cook for supper. However, when a family member comes to help us to prepare supper, our unchecked response may be somewhat impatient and critical of their help (responses related to the hyper-arousal zone in our thinking and behavioural life).

It is important to remember that our different areas of life are interrelated and we are created for *shalom* to flow throughout each. Change in one area of life may impact another area. In the example above, if our family member responds to our tetchiness with compassionate empathy – perhaps by showing that they've seen how hard this week has been for us and inviting us to take a rest while they prepare supper – we can be touched by their thoughtful actions, which lie in the wellbeing section of the Wellbeing Zone table. This will help to move our responses towards the wellbeing section too.

As humans, our lives follow a natural order of change. A natural span of life begins with conception and development in our mother's womb, followed by growth and development through childhood, adulthood and then decline in older years and finally death. Changes during a lifespan naturally bring losses and gains. Even welcomed changes bring losses too. An example is an adult's decision to marry the person they love, which also brings the loss of the freedoms of single life. To nurture wellbeing and flourishing in the different stages and seasons of life requires that we continually consider how we will change and adapt to the circumstances we find ourselves in. Part of the process of beneficial change is acceptance of losses. This can be hard to do. The practice of lament, which is honestly voicing our feelings of grief, anger, despair or regret before God and asking for his help in the situation, may provide a helpful way to process and accept a loss. We will look at the practice of lament in more detail in chapter seven.

Jesus invites us to consider change as something we can initiate. At the beginning of Jesus' teaching ministry, he gave out the invitation to humanity to "Repent, for the kingdom of heaven has come near" (Matthew 4:17, NIVUK). The word "repent" is translated from the Hebrew word *Teshuva*, which means "to return", "to change", "a transformation". To repent, therefore, is to return to a compassionate God and receive a new beginning.

The Wellbeing Zone's PEACE and PRAY models seek to be a helpful reflective tool to enable beneficial change, to consider and choose a new beginning that leads towards peace.

How spirituality is understood in the Wellbeing Zone

The word "spiritual" brings many interpretations. While there is a wide range of theological beliefs across the many Christian denominations and churches, it is generally held that Christian spirituality is the structuring of personal and community life by compassionate relationships with God, self, others and creation – our response to God's compassion made known in Jesus Christ by the Holy Spirit, as described by the American Methodist Homer Jernigan.[9] The Wellbeing Zone table and PEACE and PRAY models seek to embrace this definition as tools that can be used in individual and community contexts to foster compassionate relationships with ourselves, with others, with nature and with God (if a person is seeking a relationship with God). The PEACE and PRAY models offer a simple structure for Christians to respond to the love of God revealed in Jesus and at work through the Holy Spirit.

The Wellbeing Zone's understanding of spirituality is that it encompasses a relationship between us and the created world, including nature. Pope Francis encouraged Christians to include care of nature in their life of faith. He writes: "The ecological crisis is also a summons to profound interior conversion ... What [is needed] is an 'ecological conversion', whereby the effects of their encounter with Jesus Christ becomes evident in their relationship with the world around them. Living our vocation to be protectors of God's handiwork is essential to a life of virtue; it is not an optional or a secondary aspect of our Christian experience."[10]

While spiritualty it is often linked to religious beliefs, the Wellbeing Zone takes a broader understanding of spirituality to enable ethical, sensitive cross-cultural application in a wide variety of situations. Besides Homer Jernigan's explanation of Christian spirituality, the Wellbeing Zone also draws from these three all-encompassing descriptions of spirituality:

- The definitive principles which shape a life leading to humanity's full flourishing and profound sense of contentment. The search for supreme meaning in life.[11]

  Philip Sheldrake, a leading academic scholar on spiritualty

- "Spirituality is at the heart of individuals and communities. It motivates us and addresses questions of what we truly want for ourselves and for one another ... and [is an] important resource to mobilise people to climate change and the care of God's creation."[12]

Nick Holtam, a former UK Anglican bishop

- Spiritual health is demonstrated by how people live in harmony within the following four spheres of relationships:

    Personal – relationship with ourselves.

    Communal – relationships with others.

    Transcendental – relationship to what or to whom is beyond human level.

    Environmental – relationship with nature.[13]

    John Fisher, an Australian academic researcher on spirituality and wellbeing

Taking these descriptions on board, the Wellbeing Zone describes spiritual wellbeing as:

"Having the capacity to form and connect with core beliefs, values and sustaining practices during suffering and everyday life, which recognise self and others hold infinite worth and care of nature. Nurturing peace and wellbeing for self and all."

The Wellbeing Zone describes some key features of a spiritual life that psychological research has demonstrated lead to the nurturing of wellbeing and flourishing within individuals and communities.

These elements are: giving and receiving forgiveness; accepting mystery; seeking justice for all; holding the qualities of hope, compassion, patience, gratitude, generosity and kindness; enjoying beauty and a sense of awe and wonder; altruism. These are also characteristics of living life following Jesus' example. We will explore these spiritual qualities further in chapter eleven.

Trauma, wellbeing and the Bible

The Wellbeing Zone table offers a trauma-informed approach to wellbeing. A trauma-informed approach asks: "What has happened to you?" rather than "What is wrong with you?" or "What is your problem?" Trauma-informed care allows individuals and communities to tell their story rather than feel that they are being judged or that there is something wrong with them.

Innate to humanity is our ability to tell and hear stories. The Bible is a collection of stories with an overarching narrative. Christians understand the Bible to be God's story, covering what God wants humanity to know so that we can live well. While the word "trauma" has risen to the fore recently, the Bible, along with other religious texts and ancient myths and tales, offers humanity connection, wisdom and insight into how wellbeing may be nurtured in times of traumatic distress and suffering.[14,15]

The story of the Old Testament prophet Elijah (see 1 Kings 17 – 19) illustrates this concept well. Elijah was considered spiritually mature and someone who lived life seeking to do what he sensed God was calling him to do. He then ended up in a situation where his life was in great danger, so he fled into the desert terrified and alone. Deserts are harsh environments, offering little sustenance for life, let alone human wellbeing. The story describes God's response to Elijah's vulnerable situation. God first provided shelter for Elijah by way of a bush and then a cave. These allowed Elijah to rest and sleep. God also practically provided water, food and relational comfort through the angel's touch, which flowed from God's compassionate empathy for Elijah. Elijah was invited to tell his story and to share his experiences in order to feel understood and that God cared for him. As a prompt for Elijah to reflect on what had brought him to this state, and an invitation for Elijah to become aware of what he really needed for his wellbeing, twice God asked Elijah: "What are you doing here?" After physically, emotionally, relationally and spiritually restoring him, God then provided for Elijah's future wellbeing. God heard Elijah's comment that "I am the only one left" and responded by providing two new kings, Hazael and Jehu. God also put in place the next prophet Elisha, so Elijah no longer felt alone. When we are going through difficult or traumatic circumstances, we can feel alone in our distress. Stories of how others have journeyed through difficulties in life can bring insight, hope and connection.

Research is continually bringing new insights into how to best respond to trauma. This has led to what is called a "trauma-informed lens". The Bible may be read through a trauma-informed lens. This means including consideration of current scientific knowledge about trauma when considering sensitive application of the Bible and Christian spiritual practices in contexts where there is trauma.[16,17,18,19]

Dani, Sam, Jo and the Wellbeing Zone

After two months, Dani gradually began to trust Jo. Jo was completely different from the people who had trafficked her. With Jo, she felt a sense of being valued as a person through the warmth and kindness she experienced. She had been wary of Jo at first, but seeing Jo's consistent, respectful, humble way of relating to others – both colleagues and the other people whom the charity helped – enabled Dani to begin to feel able to share her experiences of what had happened to her. As Dani shared her personal story with Jo, Dani began to make sense of some of the things that had happened to her, including the enormity of what she had lost over the past few years.

When Jo was first introduced to Dani, Jo noticed Dani looked tired and seemed in poor health. She seemed emotionally low and flat, sitting in a withdrawn posture and reluctant to talk with Jo and others. When Jo asked what drink Dani would like, Dani replied quietly that she "didn't know". Jo noted that these observations about Dani lay within the hypo-arousal zone of the Wellbeing Zone table.

Towards the end of Jo's first meeting with Dani, Jo noticed a shift in Dani as she became anxious and seemed on edge when Jo reminded Dani that the centre was closing shortly for the evening. Jo was aware Dani's anxiety evoked feelings of anxiety within herself too. As Jo recollected to herself that several other clients had initially presented in a similar way but were now beginning to make changes after engaging with the support the organisation offered, notably with their physical health through accessing medical care and by developing supportive relationships with others, Jo was able to ground herself, enabling her emotional and thinking life to move back into the wellbeing (green) zone. Through Jo's gentle, calm voice and her sharing that she sensed Dani seemed anxious when Jo said that the afternoon session was drawing to a close, Dani felt able to reveal to Jo her anxiety about her traffickers finding her on the way home. This was a familiar concern of many clients. Jo listened to Dani's fears and shared what the organisation and police advised to help Dani to be and feel safe.

On her way home, Jo recollected that initially when she began working with the charity, she was aware she felt anxious and guilty when closing the centre and watching the clients leave. In the evenings, she would worry about the safety and wellbeing of her clients. Jo remembered that by discussing these feelings and thoughts in supervision, she had become aware that some of them were evoked because her clients

Christian beliefs that inform the Wellbeing Zone

reminded her of her first experiences of moving to London and feeling alone and overwhelmed. Jo had found that through reflecting on the Wellbeing Zone table and through her supervisor's compassionate understanding, she was able to separate out what were her personal past experiences and what were other people's feelings. Jo had also shared with her supervisor that she had recently moved to a new flat, which had meant her life outside of work had been very busy the past week. This had resulted in her normal practice of taking time before work for an early morning run, where she had space and peace for quiet prayer and reflection, slipping. Jo had missed her uninterrupted time with God while running. The Wellbeing Zone's PEACE model had provided a structure for Jo to think through what would be a good morning routine for her, given that her commute was a little longer. She had found for several years the daily practice of a morning run and time for prayer a sustaining practice that provided a helpful foundation for the challenges of the day ahead, and so had decided to adapt her morning routine by running her commute to work and then using the centre's staff showers. This allowed Jo to return to a routine of daily quiet time with God, where she experienced God's compassion for her as she shared her concerns and needs with him. Looking after her physical and spiritual wellbeing was an important life value for Jo, and her daily runs energised her. She was aware this practice significantly contributed to her wellbeing in her emotional, thinking, behavioural and relational life too.

As Sam was walking back from work through the park a couple of weeks after his previous supervision session, Sam noticed the first signs of autumn with the leaves turning colour, and his path was scattered with fallen leaves. His conversation with his spouse about the family finances had gone well and he felt a sense of peace about the plan they had made. He remembered with fondness his mother's phrase: "God sees us and cares for us all. Father God loves you."

Sam felt grateful for his mother's nurturing of his Christian spirituality, grateful for the loving relationships he experienced with his current family and with God, and grateful for being able to enjoy the beautiful autumn early evening walking through the park. His recent readings of the Bible had helped him feel not so alone in his current struggles. He sensed a return to knowing God's compassion deep within him. Sam recognised this was a shift from his previous feelings of anxiety and being over-reactive with others. As he reflected on this change, he knew God is always compassionate, but acknowledged his feelings of anxiety sometimes got in the way of him being able to draw on the truths of his Christian faith. He was grateful for being able to return to feeling at peace with God through his spiritual practice of repentance, asking God for forgiveness and then choosing to grow in God's compassion.

Chapter 5

Counselling theories and neuroscience that inform the Wellbeing Zone

Alongside Christian theology, the Wellbeing Zone also incorporates the latest understanding of neuroscience and counselling theories, which are unpacked here. We begin this chapter with the medical term Post-Traumatic Stress Disorder and present the UK Government's current definition of trauma and the features of trauma-informed care.

Post-Traumatic Stress Disorder

In Western medicine, the concept of psychological trauma was first cited in *The Diagnostic and Statistical Manual of Mental Disorders* (DSM) 3 in 1980 with the term Post-Traumatic Stress Disorder (PTSD).[20] This first description of PTSD recognised a link between a "traumatic stressor", that is what has happened to a person, to the "features of distress". For readers not familiar with the DSM, it was created after the Second World War by the American Psychiatric Association to establish a unified and definitive diagnostic system for the medical care and treatment of mental ill-health. As research into mental health advances, along with changes in Western society in what is deemed normal, healthy or unhealthy, the DSM is updated with new editions. Although used globally in mental health medical care, the DSM's application in non-Western cultures has been critiqued in relation to cultural sensitivity.

In order to understand how our bodies respond to stressful or traumatic situations, we need to look at the limbic system, as it activates and regulates our innate survival responses. The limbic system is made of inter-connected structures deep within the brain and is often referred to as the body's emotional control centre. The amygdala, which are almond-sized structures in each side of our brain, are part of the limbic system. The amygdala processes what we see and hear to pick up on potential threats to our safety. Chemical and nerve signals are then activated to enable the body to optimally respond to the threat. This is when the body's hyper-arousal responses kick in. Sometimes after experiencing a traumatic event, the amygdala can become over sensitive, setting off the body's survival responses when we don't need them to be activated. This is a feature of PTSD and can be very distressing.

The functioning of the amygdala and pre-frontal cortex

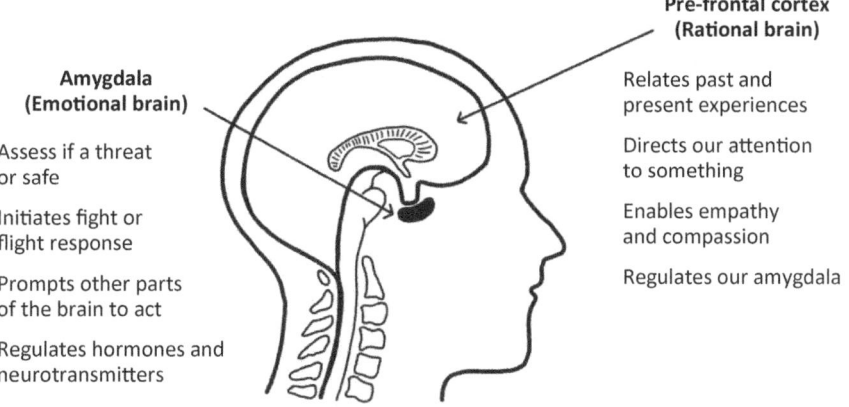

Amygdala (Emotional brain)

Assess if a threat or safe

Initiates fight or flight response

Prompts other parts of the brain to act

Regulates hormones and neurotransmitters

Pre-frontal cortex (Rational brain)

Relates past and present experiences

Directs our attention to something

Enables empathy and compassion

Regulates our amygdala

When we encounter demanding, adverse, stressful, abusive or traumatic events, hyper-arousal responses are our body's first-line survival responses. These are often called "fight" or "flight" responses. Some of the common features of fight or flight responses are described in the Wellbeing Zone table's red-coloured strand called the "hyper-arousal" zone. In stressful situations, the body's senses and nervous system pick up that there is a threat. This in turn activates the body's nerve and hormonal signals to stimulate the adrenal glands (small glands situated above each kidney) to produce the hormones adrenaline and cortisol. Adrenaline enables the body to respond to short-term intense demands, for example giving us the ability to run fast from a dangerous situation. However, we cannot maintain an adrenaline response indefinitely. Cortisol enables the body to endure long-term stress, but, over time, cortisol becomes harmful to the body. The table on the right gives an overview of the effects of adrenaline and cortisol on the body.

How adrenaline and cortisol impact the body

Adrenaline	Cortisol
Increases heart and respiratory rate and blood pressure, putting a strain on the heart.	Increases blood pressure and the risk of heart disease.
Increases glucose to bloodstream.	Increases glucose in bloodstream, reduces glucose to cells.
Increases need to urinate and empty bowels.	Suppresses digestive, reproductive and growth processes, reduces libido.
Provides an energy boost.	Disrupts sleep cycles, causing fatigue.
Can cause a person to feel nervous, dizzy, on edge.	Mood swings: anxiety, depression, irritability.
Increases blood flow to brain and major muscles giving an increased strength and performance.	Muscle weakness, tension, pain, impaired recovery from exercise.
Causes shaking, trembling.	Can cause osteoporosis.
Can cause weight loss.	Can cause weight gain.
Increases sweating.	May cause skin changes.
Increases a person's pain threshold.	Weakens immune system.
A loss of pre-frontal cortex regulation, which leads to decreased logical thinking, memory.	Increases risk to auto-immune diseases and cancer. Exacerbates mental health problems.
Dilates eye pupils to improve vision.	Impairs problem solving, learning, triggers an increase in headaches.

Hyper-arousal responses cannot be maintained forever. Eventually the body will exhaust its resources, and we then move into hypo-arousal responses to enable the body to rest and recover. These are sometimes called "fold" or "freeze" responses. In the Wellbeing Zone, the "hypo-arousal" zone is the blue-coloured strand.

Most of us at some point in our lives will encounter events or relationships that we experience as extremely demanding, stressful or traumatic. In most instances we will recover naturally over time, inherently drawing on our own resources and the support of those around us. PTSD is when we continue to re-experience intrusive memories and the hyper-arousal responses that were evoked in the original traumatic event. Re-experiencing memories and experiences from past traumatic events are often referred to as "flashbacks" or "being triggered". This can be highly distressing and may hinder our ability to live daily life well, both for our own wellbeing and for those around us. These hyper-arousal responses can occur within our different areas of life – physical, emotional, thinking, behavioural, relational and spiritual. It is important to remember that each person's experience is unique and that we may not experience everything described in the Wellbeing Zone table.

While the term PTSD was developed to be used in medical contexts, understanding how trauma impacts a person has led to trauma-informed understandings being applied in wider contexts. This has enabled insight into the impact of intergenerational and systemic discrimination, inequality, deprivation and abuse upon individuals and communities.

A definition of trauma

The Wellbeing Zone table offers a trauma-informed approach to facilitate understanding in how trauma impacts wellbeing and the consideration of what would be helpful to nurture wellbeing and future flourishing. "Trauma-informed" has recently become a buzzword in care and pastoral initiatives, but what does it practically mean? The UK Government offers a simple and clear description of trauma:

"Trauma results from an event, series of events, or set of circumstances that is experienced by an individual as harmful or life threatening. While unique to the individual, generally the experience of trauma can cause lasting adverse effects, limiting the ability to function and achieve mental, physical, social, emotional, or spiritual well-being." (UK Government, 2022)[21]

This description highlights the importance of a holistic approach to trauma, which is why the Wellbeing Zone table includes consideration of physical, emotional, mental (thinking), social (behavioural and relational) and spiritual wellbeing.

The UK Government also identifies six key principles that enable trauma-informed care: safety, choice, collaboration, trustworthiness, empowerment and cultural considerations. The Wellbeing Zone includes these principles of trauma-informed approaches when considering care initiatives.

Window of tolerance

The American trauma researcher Siegal developed the concept and coined the phrase "window of tolerance", which is the "window" or zone in which a person can most effectively function.[22] The window of tolerance graphically illustrates the optimum "window" of neurobiological arousal for functioning well in everyday life. This window is narrowed by adversity or trauma. Colloquially, the window of tolerance is often called the "comfort zone". While the word "tolerance" implies "resiliency", it somehow does not quite capture the fullness of *shalom*, or wellbeing as described in the Bible. Likewise, "comfort zone" somehow misses the quality of courage that compassionate noticing, reflection, curiosity and creativity require. As we've seen in chapter three, compassionate noticing, reflection, curiosity and creativity are essential for fostering wellbeing.

The window of tolerance is the green-coloured middle "wellbeing" or "befriending" strand on the Wellbeing Zone.

Hyper-arousal responses arise from activation of the body's sympathetic nervous system (often called fight-or-flight responses). Hypo-arousal responses arise from activation of the body's parasympathetic nervous system (often called rest-and-recovery responses).

How the body's two different nervous systems affect hyper- and hypo-arousal responses

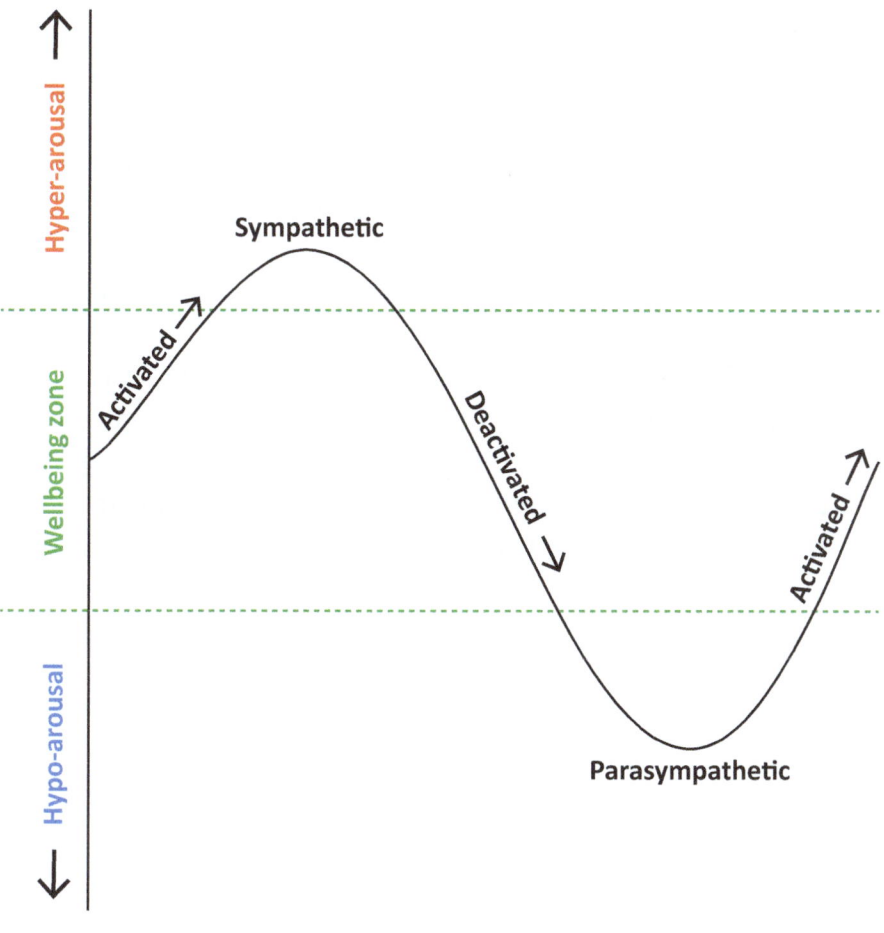

Trauma can magnify natural balance between the sympathetic and parasympathetic systems. Learning what actions kindle the sympathetic and parasympathetic nervous system offers insight into how to foster wellbeing in our everyday lives as well as when we are recovering from a significant adverse event. For example, when we are feeling very anxious, our bodies respond with hyper-arousal reactions. This may include rapid, shallow breathing and our muscles becoming tense. This prepares the body for fight-or-flight actions. However, by learning to intentionally relax our muscles and to take steady, slow, deep breaths, our body's parasympathetic system becomes activated, leading to a lowering of the sympathetic (hyper-arousal) reaction. This is an example of a grounding skill. A grounding skill is an action that enables our bodies to move from hyper-arousal responses to our wellbeing zone. Chapter six has more information on different types of grounding skills. Conversely, perhaps if we are feeling tired and sluggish in the middle of the afternoon but still have the demands of further work to be completed, taking a short break to be physically active can energise us through stimulating the sympathetic nervous system.

How the sympathetic and parasympathetic nervous systems impact the body

Sympathetic nervous system	Parasympathetic nervous system
Fight or flight	Rest and recovery
Increased heart rate	Decreased heart rate
Dilated airways	Regeneration and repair
Energy mobilisation	Energy storage
Inflammatory	Anti-inflammatory

Fight, flight, freeze, fold or befriend responses to trauma

The Wellbeing Zone also draws from the work of Janina Fisher, an American expert in the care and treatment of psychological trauma.[23] Fisher describes neurobiological reactions to traumatic events as hyper-arousal fight-or-flight responses, or hypo-arousal fold-or-freeze responses. In her work as a trauma psychotherapist, Fisher seeks to develop "befriending" responses – compassionate interventions that target the legacy of trauma. The Wellbeing Zone's green wellbeing area is named "befriending" to highlight compassion's active quality: the choice to befriend ourselves, to be compassionate to ourselves and to others.

Both Siegal and Fisher, alongside the many other neurobiological trauma experts, provide understanding and normalisation of our body's natural survival responses. By using everyday language, the Wellbeing Zone table offers a simple description of common features of survival responses. This can enable a sense of clarity and normalisation. Experiencing the signs of hyper- and hypo-arousal can leave us feeling confused as to what is going on within us. Normalisation also provides a base for compassionate responses. By using verbs, i.e. active language, the Wellbeing Zone offers pathways for change. It also broadens cross-cultural application by refraining from using Western diagnostic terms. It is important to note here that our responses may be shaped by cultural norms, which highlights the need to expand the descriptions within the Wellbeing Zone to a person's cultural context. This could be done by using the blank copy of the Wellbeing Zone table in appendix G.

Developing resiliency and new ways of coping – Lahad's "BASIC Ph" model

Mooli Lahad, an Israeli expert in care and treatment of psychological trauma, developed his "BASIC Ph" model of coping and resiliency.[24] This model offers an easy-to-remember acronym describing the different resources we innately use when faced with or seeking to recover from trauma.

Summary of Mooli Lahad's "BASIC Ph" model

B	**Beliefs:** trust in God, trust in self, trust in others, meaning, values, hope.
A	**Affect:** expressing and sharing emotions.
S	**Social:** friends, family, roles, community.
I	**Imagination:** creativity, humour, intuition, doing something different.
C	**Cognition:** information, learning, planning, self-talk, problem solving.
Ph	**Physiology:** action, relaxation, working, sports, eating, medication.

Each of us, drawing on our natural strengths and how our culture and past has equipped us, will tend to instinctively draw from one or two of the sources described. Lahad's research identified that resiliency stems from the ability to develop new ways of coping by drawing from areas within the BASIC Ph model that a person does not normally draw from. Some people will do this intuitively in the struggle to survive. For others, these skills can be developed through individual and community-based initiatives. The BASIC Ph model highlights the value of holistic, creative approaches in development of new skills to nurture wellbeing and flourishing. This echoes the Austrian Victor Frankl's observations from his experience of being imprisoned in a Nazi concentration camp during the Second World War. Frankl, a neurologist and psychologist by profession, observed that when we are no longer able to change a situation, we are challenged to change ourselves.[25] The Wellbeing Zone table and the Wellbeing Zone's PEACE and PRAY models seek to assist in the discernment of which new skills would be helpful to develop. It offers a twin-targeted holistic approach that addresses difficulties and distress, while also developing wellbeing.

Seligman's PERMA model of flourishing

While personal resilience provides the capacity to respond well to adversity, the concept of resiliency may unintentionally place a burden on the individual. This can lead to "I/you need to be more resilient" type reactions, which often evoke blame- and shame-type responses. Resiliency can also lead to pride reactions of "I am/you are resilient", which can place a weight to continue to be resilient. Pride, along with shaming and blaming responses, can inadvertently shut down compassionate reflectivity, curiosity and creativity, potentially leading to simplistic, individualistic responses that may overlook the influencing contexts, which can be complex.[26] By contrast, the Wellbeing Zone takes a "flourishing" approach. A flourishing approach invites consideration of external and environmental factors and what is conducive to both individual and collective wellbeing and flourishing. A focus on flourishing encourages holistic relational and positive outcome orientated approaches that are sensitive to others and their wellbeing and flourishing too. Martin Seligman, who was president of the American Psychological Association, presented his PERMA model of five foundational factors that contribute towards flourishing at his inaugural address.[27] The five foundational factors of the PERMA model are:

- **P**ositive emotion – enabled by cultivating gratitude, forgiveness, noticing beauty and the appreciation of joy, hope for the future.

- **E**ngagement – the experience of being fully engaged or absorbed in an activity that uses a person's skills. This can be work, caring for others, a hobby, a conversation, reading, listening to music, etc.

- **R**elationships – connection with and support from others. Doing acts of kindness for others. Developing compassionate, collaborative relationships in our personal and work lives.

- **M**eaning – a sense of meaning and purpose arising from belonging to and serving something bigger than yourself. This includes family life, a religion, a charity, a club or organisation, a community.

- **A**ccomplishment – pursuing achievement, competence and mastery. This can be in family, social or work life, a sport, a hobby.

These five factors have been shown to contribute towards health as well as sustain wellbeing. Embedded in the PERMA model is an enquiry rather than a prescriptive approach, recognising our personal uniqueness as to what enables flourishing. The Wellbeing Zone table and the Wellbeing Zone's PEACE and PRAY models embrace the PERMA model's properties.

Burnout

The term "burnout" was first conceived by the American psychologist Herbert Freudenberger.[28] Burnout describes the consequences of prolonged severe stress. Those in roles who give out to others are particularly vulnerable. Burnout impacts not only our physical wellbeing by physical exhaustion, sleep difficulties and increased vulnerability to sickness, but also our emotional, thinking, behavioural, relational and spiritual life.[29] Features of burnout are: emotional exhaustion and depletion of the capacity to be compassionate and empathic to others; negative self-evaluation, cynicism and a pervading dissatisfaction with accomplishments; increased use of addictive substances; relational detachment and increased relational personal difficulties; and spiritually, a loss of idealism and dehumanising of others. These aspects of burnout are included in the Wellbeing Zone table.

Research into burnout has highlighted the importance of self-reflective practices and the role of peers and others in early identifying of burnout.[30] The Wellbeing Zone table and the Wellbeing Zone's PRAY and PEACE models are designed to assist in reflective practices by offering a structure within which to notice and reflect compassionately and thoughtfully. They also cultivate curiosity and creativity, which fosters reflexive practice: the ability to change to enable best practice and wellbeing.

Balance and harmony

The psychology researcher Tim Lomaz puts forward that the "golden thread" in wellbeing is "balance" and "harmony".[31] Wellbeing arises out of the optimal balance and harmony in any, and ideally all, areas of life. Balance is the relationship between two interlinked phenomena. Harmony is the quality of relationships across many areas of life. The inter-relationship between balance and harmony reflects the dynamic qualities within *shalom* described within the Bible. The Wellbeing Zone table and the Wellbeing Zone's PEACE and PRAY models encourage contemplation across our six areas of life, looking at how these six areas are interlinked and how balance and harmony can be nurtured.

Post-traumatic growth

The American psychology professors Richard Tedeschi and Lawrence Calhorn coined the phrase "post-traumatic growth" to describe the positive psychological growth that can arise in the aftermath of trauma.[32] Post-traumatic growth is growth beyond our previous resilience. It is only when we are rocked to the core by a difficult or traumatic experience that post-traumatic growth can happen. In post-traumatic growth, we are changed. We have had to adapt and modify our beliefs to take into account the traumatic experience. It is the struggle with the new reality that enables post-traumatic growth. The Wellbeing Zone includes the five spheres of post-traumatic growth that Tedeschi and Calhorn's research identified:

- **Deeper appreciation of life.** When we have confronted loss and fear we can become better at noticing and valuing what we do have.
- **Warmer and more intimate relationships** through the need to give and receive support.

- **Increased sense of personal strength.** Feeling better equipped to face future challenges.

- **Awareness of new possibilities in life.** We learn to adapt and innovate with the new reality of the impact of the trauma.

- **Positive spiritual development.** Trauma challenges our core beliefs about ourselves, about others, about the world and our beliefs about God. This includes the important questions of what gives us meaning and purpose in life and the values that we seek to live by.

Their research found that post-traumatic growth often happens naturally. However, Tedeschi discovered post-traumatic growth can be facilitated by five activities,[33] which the Wellbeing Zone seeks to facilitate:

- **Education** – how trauma impacts us, what we have learned from the experience and what may be helpful responses.

- **Emotional regulation** – learning to be able to regulate emotions so we no longer feel overwhelmed by fear and distress. This can include learning how to regulate mis-projected anger.

- **Disclosure** – thoughtful sharing of experiences with others about what has happened and what we are now struggling with.

- **Narrative development** – being able to tell the story about the trauma and how we will live afterwards in a meaningful way. Recognising that the trauma was in the past and from it we are now shaping a better future.

- **Serving or helping others** – our experience and growth following trauma may bring insightful encouragement to others who are similarly affected.

Trauma-informed care is complex and multi-faceted, requiring a steady, compassionate approach to equip the person, and those around them, with the skills to nurture wellbeing and flourishing. For integrative trained counsellors and counsellors in training, the Wellbeing Zone aids in the consideration of which counselling or psychological approaches and interventions may be helpful at any given time. This can include discussing with the person referrals to specialist psychological and medical professionals.

Principles of safety for conversations about trauma

The Wellbeing Zone facilitates a trauma-informed approach. We have seen in the previous chapter that a trauma-informed approach is a "What has happened to me?", "What has happened to you?" way of responding. Trauma-informed care allows individuals and communities to tell their story rather than feel that they are being judged or that there is something wrong with them.

Part of post-traumatic growth following trauma is being able to tell our story about the trauma. This can be difficult. For someone who has experienced trauma, telling their story or answering questions can trigger memories from the traumatic experience. These trauma memories may be acutely distressing and re-traumatising. A "flashback" may be induced. A flashback is when something in the past feels as though it is happening in the present. Not only is this distressing, but it may increase the risk of developing PTSD.

Our recollection of a past event is based upon our cognitive ability at the time of the event. When a person is talking about what has happened in their childhood, their memories of the event will be shaped by their age at the time.

As we have seen, when we experience a traumatic event, the front part of our brain that stores memories and solves problems (the pre-frontal cortex) gets bypassed by the body's survival response. This enables automatic responses, which are quicker, rather than thinking through what to do in the middle of an emergency. That is why we practise fire drills and first aid, so we instinctively know what to do. When the pre-frontal cortex part of the brain goes offline, the original memory of the event may not be formed as a clear, sequential story. This can result in memories being fragmented, confused and having parts missing. Trying to form a coherent full picture of what happened can lead to further distress. Instead, a compassionate acceptance that there may be some parts in a traumatic experience that will be unable to be remembered and may never resurface paves the way for creating a story about the traumatic event that the mind can store away. This is important, so that the trauma event then becomes something that happened in the past, enabling the mind to be free to focus on living in the present. For example, someone who has had a car crash may remember they signalled to turn right and then the next thing they remember is the car airbag inflating in front of them. The actual crash cannot be remembered because their body's survival responses were in action. The story would therefore be, "I turned right, then I can't remember what happened as the next thing I recall is the car airbag inflating in front of me."

Research has identified five foundational principles for the effective prevention of PTSD.[34] These principles provide a helpful framework when considering conversations with someone who may have experienced trauma. The five principles are:

- **Promoting a sense of safety**

    Consider carefully what needs to be put in place so everyone feels safe.

    Ask the person if there is anything you need to be aware of or anything they would like in place beforehand.

    Explain the reasons behind anything you do.

    Be collaborative and respectful and explain that you will go at the pace that is comfortable for the other person.

- **Promoting calmness**

    This may include:

    - explaining our typical reactions to traumatic events
    - developing problem-solving skills to nurture the ability to evaluate a situation realistically
    - developing self-care skills when we notice we are moving out of the Wellbeing Zone.

- **Promoting a sense of personal and collective efficacy**

    This is the belief in the ability to recover well.

    What does the person and their community need practically?

    Consider what skills and resources are needed to do this.

- **Promoting relational connectedness**

    Nurturing relationships that are compassionate, respectful, collaborative and accountable, and where all can flourish.

    Cultivating a broad range of relationships for support, connection, sharing and enjoying life with.

- **Instilling hope**

    Conversations, support and activities that create realistic hope.

    Noticing where there is hope, even if it is tiny, and building on that hope.

When seeking to prevent secondary trauma, these three things have been found to be helpful:[35]

- **First, do no harm.** Consider the consequences of a potential action or initiative so unintended harm is avoided.

- **Refrain from pathologising** (labelling problems or difficulties). Instead, explain what normal reactions to abnormal (traumatic) events are.

- **Refrain from psychologising** (increasing emotional reactions, reinforcing the memory through detailed questioning). Instead focus on the five principles described above.

Counselling theories and neuroscience that inform the Wellbeing Zone

When using the Wellbeing Zone, it is important to allow sufficient time for the person to tell their story at their pace and in the detail that they feel safe to share. By both the listener and storyteller understanding how trauma can impact the ability to share a story of what has happened, re-traumatisation can be prevented. Taking considerations so that a person is in the wellbeing zone as they tell their story, noticing any movement towards the margins of the wellbeing zone, and, if so, pausing and reconsidering how to maintain being in their wellbeing zone results in the story being stored in the brain as something that has happened in the past.

All of the above can be utilised when thinking about how to support your own wellbeing, or the wellbeing of those you work with – see appendix D and the example below.

An organisation's approach to trauma-informed care using the Wellbeing Zone

The organisation that Sam and Jo work for provides initial training for new staff to equip them to deliver trauma-informed care and support for their clients. The organisation recognises that their staff are exposed to secondary trauma through listening to their clients' traumatic experiences and so all staff receive regular training on trauma-informed care and support of supervision to foster their personal wellbeing and also the wellbeing of their clients.

The charity strives for a culture of care for their staff and welcomes suggestions from both staff and clients on what would cultivate flourishing. The staff find the reflective skills they learn in psychological supervision, through reflecting on the Wellbeing Zone table and the Wellbeing Zone's team and personal plans they created at a staff wellbeing workshop, cultivates a culture of compassionate care for each other's wellbeing. This happens through noticing when a team member's margins of wellbeing have been reached and they are beginning to show early signs of compassion fatigue, burnout or secondary trauma. Taking time to discuss what would be helpful to restore wellbeing by using the Wellbeing Zone's PEACE model promotes a sense of personal and collective efficacy, restoring calmness and harmony to the organisation's culture, alongside promptly responding with care to individual or group features of secondary trauma. The staff found creating the Wellbeing Zone team plan (see appendix D) stimulated lots of conversations and ideas on what they could do during the working day and during their break times as well as making changes to the staff room.

Recent initiatives to foster organisational flourishing have included: creating a photography workshop so people could tell their stories and express their feelings and their hopes for the future through photographs that were curated into an artistic display in the centre's main room; turning the small patch of grass at the back of the building into a vegetable and flower garden, which staff and clients can harvest; and staff being given contracted wellbeing days to enable them to take a day off work to care for their personal wellbeing when needed. Staff have found the wellbeing days contribute towards a sense of balance, especially in very busy times, or when they are feeling emotionally depleted from giving out to their clients.

Dani's reflections on the impact of the garden mirrored other clients' reflections, with common themes including: their gratitude for the organisation listening to their suggestions; the enjoyment of noticing changes each week as the plants grew; being engaged with a shared task, with the sense of accomplishment of creating a garden where others would also find benefit; and being able to have something to give to others such as a small bunch of fresh herbs, flowers or freshly picked vegetables.

Embedded in the organisation's policies, procedures and range of support services offered to clients are the trauma-informed care principles of safety, choice, collaboration, trustworthiness, empowerment and cultural considerations. The organisation has clear safeguarding policies and regular training in safeguarding as their client group is made up of vulnerable adults. At both an organisational and ground level (the daily practical support initiatives that the charity offers clients), the physical and psychological safety of clients and staff is considered. There is transparency in decision-making to foster trust within the organisation and with clients. Decisions are made collaboratively, with staff and client's strengths being recognised, developed and honoured. Through education in how trauma and secondary trauma may impact clients and staff, and likewise understanding how post-traumatic growth can be nurtured, clients and staff are empowered to nurture their healing and wellbeing. The staff team reflect the cultural diversity of the local area and consideration is given to respectfully understanding each client's culture, with support initiatives being culturally sensitive to enable belonging. All the initiatives have a trauma-informed focus on nurturing wellbeing and encouraging and supporting post-traumatic growth.

You will have noticed this section has focused on the organisation rather than the three individuals. This is because an individual's personal wellbeing, ability to restore from the impact of trauma and work optimally with those who have experienced trauma are all influenced by the environment that they are in. By communities and organisations taking action to ensure that trauma-informed care is integrated into every aspect of their ways of working, the environment for individual and personal wellbeing and flourishing is created.

Chapters six to eleven will focus in turn on each area of life within the Wellbeing Zone: chapter six on our physical life, chapter seven on our emotional life and so on until we reach chapter eleven and our spiritual life. In each chapter, we will look at how demanding situations or trauma may impact each of our life areas and what we can do to nurture our wellbeing. This will be illustrated by Dani's, Jo's and Sam's stories.

Chapter 6

Physical wellbeing

Physical life		
HYPER-AROUSAL ZONE Fight-or-flight response	**WELLBEING ZONE** Befriending response	**HYPO-AROUSAL ZONE** Freeze-or-fold response
Increase in adrenaline; raised heart and breathing rate, blood redirected to muscles, shaking; surge in energy then exhaustion; activation of neurobiological survival responses; increasing vulnerability to stress-related health conditions and diseases; difficulties in sleeping.	Proactive to physical health needs; sense of strength, alertness and energy as health allows.	Exhaustion; lethargy; fatigue; burnout; rundown; neglecting or struggling to be proactive in attending to physical health needs; vulnerable to sickness.

The World Health Organisation (WHO) was formed over 75 years ago with the vision to promote health as a global fundamental human right for all. The WHO's definition of health is "a complete physical, mental and social well-being and not merely the absence of disease".[36] Physical wellbeing lays the foundation for:

- wellbeing and flourishing throughout our different life areas
- wellbeing and flourishing in our other aspects of life, for example economic and social
- healthy childhood development
- prevention of diseases.

The different seasons of life bring different demands and vulnerabilities to our physical wellbeing. Naturally, the needs of a growing child are different from an adult in older age. Throughout life, our physical health requires healthy patterns of sleep, rest and exercise, balanced nutrition according to our body's needs and the maintaining of a healthy body weight. Making use of preventive healthcare provision, alongside seeking treatment and care for any medical conditions, is important for physical health. Our environment impacts our physical health, underlining the importance of community infrastructure and initiatives that support optimum physical health. Examples of these include access to a clean water supply and safe housing. Sound environmental care benefits our physical wellbeing by protecting us from the extreme forces of nature.

Our physical and mental health are directly related. Physical health problems increase the risk of mental health difficulties and vice versa. Physical wellbeing may be overlooked in survival modes of living. This can arise from current or past stress or abuse, or a lack of work-life balance. Trauma can be somatised, which means that psychological distress manifests itself in our physical health. A common form of this is when we experience a painful headache during a stressful day. However, if we are living with prolonged traumatic psychological distress, our physical health can be severally harmed by long-term high cortisol levels.[37] Our neurobiological survival responses are at risk of becoming chronically activated too.[38] Neurobiological interventions targeted at somatised trauma hold the potential to help ease specific physical distress, alongside nurturing our wellbeing in our other life areas. These neurobiological interventions include grounding skills.

Grounding skills

Grounding skills are techniques that help us be in the present moment with a sense of emotional balance.

Grounding skills help us:

- remain in the wellbeing zone when we sense we are moving towards the edges of our wellbeing zone and into either the hyper- or hypo-arousal zones

- move towards the wellbeing zone when we notice that we are in the hyper- or hypo-arousal zones.

In the previous chapter we saw that hyper-arousal responses arise from activation of the body's sympathetic nervous system (often called fight-or-flight responses) and that hypo-arousal responses arise from activation of the body's parasympathetic nervous system (often called rest-and-recovery responses).

Grounding skills help us to move out of the hyper-arousal zone and towards the green wellbeing zone. Grounding skills are things we can do to activate our parasympathetic nervous system. They are befriending skills – the choice to be compassionate to ourselves and to be compassionate to others through doing things that cultivate our and others' wellbeing. Using the PEACE or PRAY models, learn what you find most helpful for you. Be creative – there are lots of different ways to nurture our wellbeing. Below are suggestions of things you might like to try.

Relaxation breathing

There are lots of different ways of doing this. Find a pattern of breathing in through your nose slowly while counting in your mind and then breathing out through your mouth slowly, counting in your mind. Find the length of breath that works for you. Perhaps begin with four or five counts and then adjust to what enables you to feel calm and comfortable. Try to take steady breaths that flow down to your tummy. The pattern of breathing can be adjusted by breathing in for the count of four, holding your breath for the count of four, breathing out for the count of four, then holding the out breath for the count of four, and then repeating this cycle if it feels comfortable for you. Repeat or adjust this pattern until you find you are feeling calmer and in your wellbeing zone. It may take five or more minutes of relaxation breathing to bring a sense of calm when feeling particularly panicky.

Give yourself a butterfly hug

Cross your arms in front of you and place your hands on your shoulders, so the left hand is on the right shoulder and the right hand is on the left shoulder. Then gently let your hands move down your arms to your elbows, then back up and keep repeating until you feel calmer.

Actively engage your five senses in the present moment

You can do this by:

- **Sight** – say five things you can see. Notice the details, for example the dark wooden clock on the wall, the green leaf patterned curtains, the red armchair, the green and red patterned cushion, the glass side table.

- **Hearing** – say four things you can hear. For example, "I can hear the traffic of cars outside, the ticking of the wooden clock on the wall, people talking in the next room, the radio music in the background."

- **Touch** – say three things you can touch (and touch them while you are speaking). For example, "I can feel the soft velvet fabric of the red chair, the wool jumper I am wearing feels warm and soft, the fabric of my jeans feel stretchy."

- **Smell** – say two things you can smell. For example, "I can smell the soap that I used to wash my hands, I can smell the traffic fumes."

- **Taste** – say one thing you can taste. For example, "I can taste in my mouth [the last thing you ate]."

Wellbeing box

If we find we frequently move out of our wellbeing zone, it can be helpful to create a wellbeing box of things that cultivate our wellbeing, rather like having a first-aid box.

When deciding what to put in the box, choose things that nurture your wellbeing, involving your five senses. For example, for sight you could include photos of happy memories, pictures of favourite places; for hearing you could have playlists of music that lifts your soul or makes you feel joyful; for touch you could have things that hold a special significance for you, such as a shell or stone from a favourite beach; for smell perhaps a scented hand cream or candle; taste could be a favourite non-alcoholic drink or snack that can be stored. The box could include things that you can do that you find foster your overall wellbeing, such as a pack of cards, gardening gloves as a reminder to do gardening, a list of activities that you know help you feel well (go for a swim at the local pool, walk around your local park and take time to notice and appreciate the plants and trees in the park, go to a favourite café where you know you will be given a warm welcome, go to a club or group or an organised activity that you enjoy).

Engage your mind in the present

Doing a healthy, pleasant activity that engages your mind in the present moment will aid grounding, such as reading a book, doing a hobby or a sport, making a warm drink or healthy snack, listening to music that you find shifts your emotions positively, going for a walk, doing a household or admin chore that requires your concentration.

Reach out

Reach out to a friend, family member, colleague or listening organisation with whom you can share your current struggles.

Recognise and challenge unhelpful thinking with compassionate thoughts

Inspiring, encouraging, wise or thoughtful words or phrases can be helpful to ground ourselves. For those following a religion, this may include words, prayers or promises from religious texts. In chapter eight, we will look at how we can nurture our thinking wellbeing.

A holistic approach

To conclude, the Wellbeing Zone highlights that physical wellbeing is nurtured by proactive choices, supporting optimum physical health not only individually but also for others. There is a vast array of resources including books, apps, websites, videos, programmes, classes, national or local community organisations and groups which support and encourage physical wellbeing. The Wellbeing Zone's PEACE and PRAY models invite the consideration of resources and choices that foster physical wellbeing. Our physical health can be impacted by our emotional, thinking, behavioural, relational and spiritual life areas. Making changes to nurture our physical health can be challenging to initiate and maintain, particularly when it is impacted by economic, geographical and social factors. The Wellbeing Zone therefore enables a holistic consideration of physical health.

Dani, Sam, Jo and physical wellbeing

Here's a recap of what we have already learned about Dani's, Sam's and Jo's physical wellbeing:

Dani is female and in her mid-20s. Dani finds it hard to fall asleep when she goes to bed at night and her sleep is poor due to restlessness. Her poor sleep is contributing to her feeling constantly tired. Dani's nutrition is poor, due to her lack of appetite and finding the food available at her local supermarket so different compared to her food market back home. Apart from walking to appointments, Dani does no physical exercise as she is fearful of going outside of her accommodation. Dani has had a run of chest infections that take a while to heal.

Sam is male and in his mid-50s. He is in good health, and his main exercise is walking to and from work. However, he has been feeling exhausted and lacking in energy since taking on the extra taxi driver work at weekends.

Jo is female and in her early 30s. We've seen in chapter four that nurturing her physical wellbeing is an important life value for Jo and that this provides a helpful foundation for fostering her wellbeing in the other aspects of her life. She is in good health and her daily pattern of early morning runs is important for cultivating her wellbeing.

Looking at the Wellbeing Zone, we can see Jo's physical health is clearly in the green-coloured wellbeing zone. Dani's physical life meets the description in the blue-coloured hypo-arousal zone, while Sam's seems in the green-coloured wellbeing zone, apart from his exhaustion which is a feature of the blue-coloured hypo-arousal zone. This suggests that Sam's health is beginning to move out of the wellbeing zone and into the hypo-arousal zone, probably due to the demands of working at weekends. By noticing when we are moving out of the wellbeing zone, we can take prompt action to nurture our wellbeing back into the wellbeing zone. Sam was able to do this by discussing his wellbeing with his spouse and, through making a shared decision, they created a pattern of family life that supported everyone's wellbeing. Sam cut back his taxi work to one Saturday every fortnight, which enabled him to rest on the other weekend days.

Dani's physical health needs were more complex to address. Through the support Jo gave Dani, Dani was able to learn how to access her local health services so that she could receive medical treatment for her chest infections. Through attending the wellbeing group each week, Dani began to learn about how to look after her physical health. Dani was aware that since the war broke out, she had fallen into a pattern of neglecting her physical health, which worsened when she was trafficked. She couldn't remember eating a fresh vegetable or fruit during her journey to the UK. In the wellbeing group, Dani learned more about the nutritional value of the foods available in the UK. Jo then accompanied Dani to the local supermarket and pointed out which foods were both economical and nutritious. Dani also found the group discussions provided ideas on simple, healthy meals to prepare. By trying to eat regular meals and including using some of the herbs and vegetables grown in the charity's garden, Dani began to take an interest in food again and noticed her long-running chest infections were starting to heal with antibiotic treatment. The wellbeing group celebrated the different traditional cultural festivals of the clients and staff and Dani enjoyed trying the special foods of each tradition. She also enjoyed preparing her favourite dish, which her grandmother taught her to cook.

Others in the wellbeing group also struggled with sleep difficulties. Dani found the supportive conversations at the group helped her feel less alone, and therefore less anxious at night. Jo taught her several grounding skills, including relaxation breathing. Dani found doing the relaxation breathing at night and when she felt anxious helped her feel calmer. Dani would breathe in for the count of four, hold her breath for the count of four, then breathe out for the count of four, and then hold her breath again for the count of four and then repeat this cycle until she began to feel she had regained her sense of feeling steady and composed. She also found listening to music helped shift her feelings of anxiety.

Dani learned a few yoga-type movements from her wellbeing group. She found the stretching and relaxation movements not only helped her feel less achy and more relaxed, but she began to notice and want to care for her body more. Jo noticed that Dani was beginning to be more proactive about looking after her physical health.

Chapter 7

Emotional wellbeing

Emotional life		
HYPER-AROUSAL ZONE Fight-or-flight response	**WELLBEING ZONE** Befriending response	**HYPO-AROUSAL ZONE** Freeze-or-fold response
Increasing anxiety, stress, panic, frustration or mis-projected anger. Feeling restless, on-edge, overwhelmed or unsafe; over-reactive; emotional flooding.	Awareness, acceptance and understanding of feelings; being able to respond to emotions that enables wellbeing of self and others; feelings correspond to the situation; compassion; gratitude; hope; empathic to self and others; sense of inner peace.	Feeling low, flat, self-absorbed, depressed, or numb; feelings of shame, disconnection, isolation, helplessness, losing hope; feeling depleted and struggling to be compassionate to self and others; struggling to sense reality and a vulnerability to disconnect from reality.

Emotional wellbeing arises out of the ability to be aware of, accept and understand our own emotional life and that of others, and then respond in ways that nurture wellbeing and flourishing for ourselves and for others. Foundational to emotional wellbeing is compassion, as this enables empathic and kind responses.

Trauma and learning to nurture emotional wellbeing

Trauma can evoke strong emotions. Emotions that feel big, painful, confusing or overwhelming can be frightening to acknowledge. The thoughtful use of grounding skills (chapter six has some examples), taking time to nurture compassionate, safe relationships and using language that conveys empathy but does not re-traumatise are important. Acknowledging emotions requires courage and honesty as our emotional life reveals our vulnerability, our needs, our desires, and our limitations. Learning to name what we are feeling emotionally lays a pathway for growing in understanding and caring for our emotional life. Learning how to regulate our emotional life enables a sense of *shalom* within us. This emotional sense of *shalom* can be present when we are feeling emotional distress that relates to the situation we are in.

During childhood, we learn to become aware of and how to respond to our emotional life. This learning can be through planned learning activities or through adults sharing their own emotional life, but mostly it occurs through the infant and child taking in what is modelled to them by their relationships with others. Culture and significant life events, alongside how carers respond to their own emotional lives, shape the child's ability to be aware of their own emotional life. The child learns what emotions are permissible to be expressed and how, and what emotions are not to be acknowledged or expressed. Some cultures, families or individuals can overlook or avoid distressing emotions. When family life becomes too preoccupied with other things, for example parents' long working hours, attending to the emotional wellbeing of children can be overlooked. A carer may not have learned the skills for emotional wellbeing in their own childhood or may have unprocessed trauma from the past or current trauma that is impacting their life, which indirectly impacts the child.

If we avoid or overlook our emotional life, or haven't learned the skills of emotional awareness, our emotions can lie buried and disowned or be projected onto others. Emotional suppression over time leads to emotional repression. This can be a conscious or unconscious response. A conscious decision to supress an emotion can be helpful short-term, for example waiting until we are with someone we trust to share what we are feeling when a painful or difficult experience has happened. However, habitually overlooking or avoiding our emotional life leads to difficulties. Our other areas of life may be drawn towards hyper- or hypo-arousal responses as a result. It is hard work repressing strong emotions, particularly feelings of anger and anxiety. Over time we become exhausted, and this can lead to feeling low in mood. Repressed emotions can leak out when we don't want or expect them to, leading to emotional or behavioural responses that may not be helpful to our or others' wellbeing. An example of this is when we have had a really stressful or difficult day at work and then are irritable with those we are living with who have done nothing to harm or annoy us.

Different seasons of life bring different challenges, including times of uncertainty, difficulty, loss and trauma. Emotions give us insight into ourselves and how we are experiencing life, as well as our inner needs and desires. The Wellbeing Zone's PEACE and PRAY models offer a structure to become aware of and reflect on our emotional life. If we are unaware of our emotions and don't take time to attend to our emotional life in a healthy way, we can find that our behaviours are reactive and being driven by unconscious emotions. This can result in a lack of wellbeing for ourselves and for others. We are affected by the emotional life of those around us, as we pick up others' emotions. This can lead us to then feel what they are feeling. Emotional awareness enables us to distinguish between our own emotions and the emotions of others, which lays the foundation for compassionate empathic responses.

Compassionate emotional awareness provides a base from which to consider how best to attend to our and others' emotional lives. Examples of attending to our emotional lives include taking time to grieve following a loss, doing relaxation skills when feeling anxious or seeking forgiveness when we may have hurt others.

The Wellbeing Zone's wheel of emotions

The American psychologist Robert Plutchik understood that emotions are adaptive responses as they help us to survive the challenges that life brings.[39] Plutchik developed a wheel of emotions in the 1980s to assist in the learning of emotional awareness. In the wheel, emotions are paired with opposites to enable reflection on the inter-relationship between different emotions and their strength of arousal. Plutchik's wheel has been adapted by many over the years.

The Wellbeing Zone's own wheel of emotions offers a tool to enable self-awareness of some of the emotions described within the hyper-arousal, hypo-arousal and wellbeing zones and then thoughtful consideration of what would be helpful to nurture wellbeing. Often, we may be experiencing several different emotions about a situation. Taking time to identify these different emotions and their particular qualities provides a foundation to consider compassionate responses that enable:

- the healthy processing of emotions, especially emotions that we may find distressing or difficult to process. For example, feelings of anger when we have been hurt by another's actions, feelings of sadness following a significant bereavement, feelings of despair when our efforts to help others are not making the impact we would like

- learning from the insight that our emotional life offers us. For example, learning what brings us a sense of peace when we are wrestling with a difficult decision, or what the roots of feelings of anxiety are, so that we make choices that foster our wellbeing when our safety is or feels threatened

- consideration of the magnitude of how we have been impacted by something.

Processing an emotion involves learning to understand, make sense of and respond in a way that enables personal wellbeing and the consideration of the wellbeing of others.

The wheel of emotions

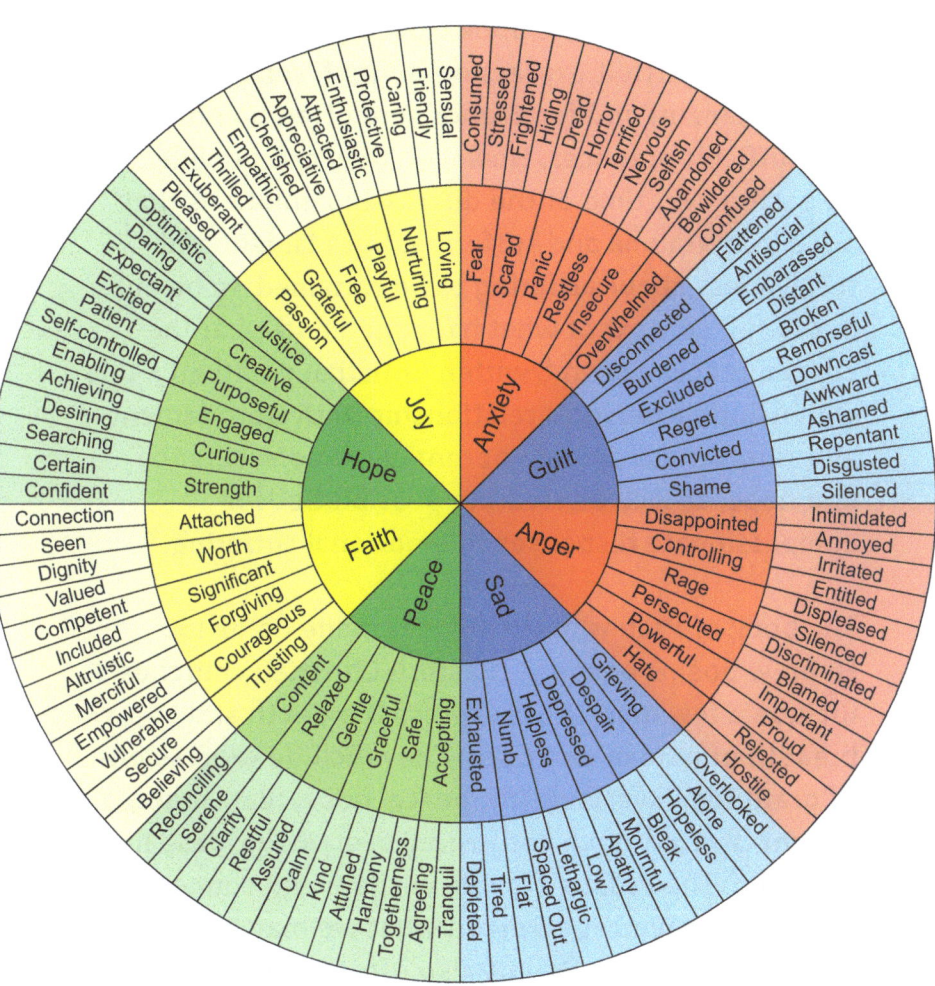

Nurturing emotional wellbeing and Christian spirituality

Emotional wellbeing doesn't mean feeling happy all the time. The only book in the Bible that is named after an emotion is the book Lamentations. Lament is a deep, heartfelt expression of grief, sorrow or regret. Lament and forgiveness are often painful and difficult practices. However, they can provide an easing over time of the distressing emotions that arise from trauma and suffering. Both lament and forgiveness allow suffering to be reframed, to be put in the full context of what happened and what the consequences are and, within Christian spiritualty, this will include a person's relationship with God. Lament and forgiveness provide potential for perseverance and hope, as well as creating possibilities for compassionate responses to emotional suffering.[40]

The book of Psalms in the Bible is made up of 150 Hebrew poems or songs (Eastern Christian churches include a few more) that express the depth and breadth of human emotions. They include expressions of gratitude, awe, love, joy, peace, hope, fear, anger, lament, sorrow, guilt, confusion, overwhelm, despair and grief. The Psalms provide wisdom and connection; others too have experienced what we may be experiencing.[41] The Psalms also offer a language and structure within which to name, express and process our emotional life. The American Old Testament theologian Walter Brueggemann describes the Psalms as having a three-part sequence of orientation, disorientation and then reorientation.[42] This three-part pattern enables a supportive structure within which to name and express the many emotions evoked when we encounter trauma. These Psalms also offer a pathway to a reorientation, to life after the trauma – to a post-traumatic growth.

The practice of gratitude has been shown to be a beneficial coping behaviour during suffering as well as fostering emotional wellbeing.[43,44] Gratitude is a feature of post-traumatic growth. In times of suffering, it is easy to overlook what we *do* have. Taking time to notice what we have is the first step in the practice of gratitude. This includes gratitude for others and how they are contributing to our wellbeing in some way, gratitude for the gift of nature and the earth's resources and gratitude for the gift of life. The practice of gratitude aids flourishing through the appreciation of other people, focusing on the positive, on what a person does have, and so helps in the formation and strengthening of relationships. Gratitude also includes the ability to express awe when noticing beauty, both in nature and in the creative arts. Gratitude helps us to form a truer perspective.

Dani, Sam and emotional wellbeing

From Dani and Sam's stories so far, we've learned that Dani's emotional life held many distressing and anxious feelings that at times she found overwhelming and confusing. Sam, on the other hand, has generally felt content in his emotional life, but recently has begun to feel anxious about his family's and the charity's finances. Alongside feeling less cheerful and optimistic, his emotional balance has become unsettled through taking on the painful emotions of those around him. We've seen in chapter two how Sam's anxious feelings were impeding his ability to think clearly. We also saw how relaxation breathing helped bring a sense of calm, enabling Sam to be able to stand back and fully consider his current situation and create a pathway forward, which hopefully will nurture both his and his family's wellbeing. We can also see the link between his feelings of frustration and anxiety and the moral injury of implementing the decisions related to the freeze in funding. Remembering Sam's walk in the park after work, we sense Sam knows that appreciating the beauty in nature brings him joy. Also, when Sam remembers and names what he is grateful for, it enables him to reconnect with the relationships and times in his life where his wellbeing is nurtured.

Anyone who has gone through what Dani went through will have experienced many highly distressing emotions. Dani struggled with feeling confused and overwhelmed, swinging from feeling anxious to feeling very low and numb. Through Jo taking time to allow Dani to trust her and Jo's calm, gentle manner and use of empathic and simple language that conveyed to Dani that Jo understood the enormity of what she had been through, Dani felt safe to begin to share her emotional life. Jo refrained from emotive, descriptive language, and this enabled Dani to slowly share her experiences without becoming overwhelmed. Dani had lost so much. Over many months, she was gradually able to express her grief and her lament as well as her hope for justice for her and her family. Through this, Dani began to be able to frame her experiences. Initially, Dani had blamed her father for his naivety in letting the traffickers take her. However, she began to realise that he had no other option. She knew he would be anxious for her welfare, and gradually her feelings of anger and blame moved towards acceptance, compassion and forgiveness. Dani found the Wellbeing Zone's PEACE model helpful as it enabled her to develop her ability to ask questions for herself. She was surprised by how much she was learning about herself, as previously she had found it hard to talk about her emotional life.

Chapter 8

Thinking wellbeing

Thinking life		
HYPER-AROUSAL ZONE Fight-or-flight response	**WELLBEING ZONE** Befriending response	**HYPO-AROUSAL ZONE** Freeze-or-fold response
Becoming focused on past and/or future events; losing perspective; self-absorbed; struggling to think clearly, remember, make decisions or mind going blank or going around in circles; becoming obsessive, judgemental and rigid; catastrophising; narrative may be inconsistent, confusing or incomplete. Distressing memories, intrusive images.	Able to think clearly, objectively and realistically; consider others' perspective and own; thinking is open to new ideas and information; problem solving; able to be reflective; curious and creative; able to give an understandable consistent narrative.	Dwelling on the past and/or future; becoming pulled towards a negative focus, fixed positions, self-absorbed; cynicism; struggling to think clearly, make decisions or going blank; going around in circles; narrative may be inconsistent, confusing, incomplete; vulnerability to dissociate from reality.

When we move into the hypo- or hyper-arousal zones, our thinking life begins to change to enable survival. When we are in the hyper- or hypo-arousal zones, our thinking patterns can become focused on the future or on the past. The capacity for creative problem solving can become reduced. Our mind can feel full of thoughts that go round in circles; our thinking becomes preoccupied. Mindfulness practices can help us become aware of our thought life and develop the ability to observe our thoughts.[45,46]

The American psychiatrist Aaron Beck, who developed Cognitive Behavioural Therapy (CBT), understood that hyper- and hypo-arousal thinking patterns reinforce hypo- or hyper-arousal responses in our other areas of life.[47] Beck saw that how an event is interpreted, rather than the event itself, can be the cause of much mental suffering.

Our brains are constantly seeking to understand internal and external events. Each day we have around 70,000–100,000 automatic thoughts. That's a lot of automatic thoughts! One automatic thought will trigger a chain of related automatic thoughts, and we are normally unaware of these thoughts. In contrast, on an average day we will hear about 20,000–30,000 words and speak about 7,000–20,000 words. The impact of automatic thoughts is huge. Automatic thoughts often fall into a pattern. When our thinking life is in the hypo- or hyper-arousal zone, our automatic thoughts will often have a negative and unhelpful focus. This can lead to a pattern of thoughts forming. Such patterns are called "thinking distortions". These thinking distortions lead to distress in our thinking and in our other areas of life. For example, we may interpret another's actions in a negative way that then leads to us feeling emotionally upset or angry, which in turn leads to us relationally withdrawing or being critical of the other person.

The skill of being able to compassionately observe our thinking life and identify a thinking distortion provides a base from which to either challenge, modify or refrain from responding to unhelpful thoughts, and so nurture our wellbeing. When we are feeling tired or stressed, our thinking may veer towards two or three of these common thinking distortions. Recognising which are our familiar distorted thinking patterns enables us to become more alert to when they are occurring. Learning to challenge our negative automatic thoughts with a thought that helps foster wellbeing enables our thought life to nurture our wellbeing.

In the table on page 147, the left-hand column describes different types of thinking distortions. The middle column offers a description of the thinking distortion. As you read down the left-hand and middle columns, notice which type of thinking distortions you experience more often, particularly when you are tired or feeling stressed. The right-hand column offers a way of challenging the thinking distortion. When you next notice your thoughts are following a thinking distortion, challenge the thinking distortion with the corresponding question or thought in the right-hand column.

You may find it helpful to write out the frequent thinking distortions that come into your thought life and then write out how you will challenge them. Sometimes it can be hard to challenge a thinking distortion. When this happens, do something that distracts your thinking away from the thinking distortion and instead focuses your attention on something else. For example, reading an enjoyable book, listening to music that shifts your thoughts and feelings towards joy or peace, doing an absorbing hobby or task such a housework or admin, taking the initiative to have a conversation with someone.

A table of common thinking distortions

THINKING DISTORTION	DESCRIPTION OF THE THINKING DISTORTION	RESPONDING TO THE THINKING DISTORTION
Catastrophising	Worst-case scenario thinking, scanning for every possible potential worst outcome.	Consider: what is the evidence for these potential scenarios? What is realistically most likely to happen?
Emotional reasoning	I feel it so it must be true.	Bear in mind our feelings are due to how we interpret an event, so ask: Are my interpretations accurate? Can I consider different interpretations?
Expert	Assuming what works in one situation will also work in all other situations.	Remember each situation/topic is unique; consider other people's input.
Globalising	Labelling everything or people as the same, often negatively.	Respect that everyone is unique; things are complex and made up of many parts.
Low tolerance	Magnifying the difficulties or emotional pain and minimising your coping skills.	Consider potential resources and support to enable a stepped approach to challenges.
Microscopic	Focusing on one small part, which then rules the overall outlook.	Consider the bigger picture, the wider context.
Mind-reading	Assuming others are thinking negatively about you.	Remember no one fully knows another's thoughts. Consider asking for or inviting feedback.
Minimising	To make negative impact seem smaller or less important.	Consider the full impact and consequences of the situation/event.
Negative focus	Focus on the negative and overlook the positive or what is OK in the situation.	Consider what may be the positives or the OK in the situation.
Othering	Labelling people into groups having different characteristics from you.	Honouring the unique value of each person. Being welcoming to others who may be different from you.
Personalising	Taking total responsibility or blame for distressing events.	Consider explanations that do not involve you, the bigger picture, other contributing factors or how others have contributed.
Polarised thinking	Thinking in polar opposites, something is either all good or all bad.	Recognise life is complex, rarely is something all good or all bad. Remember good can come out of bad situations, and good things can have negative parts.
Quickest route	Focusing only on the quickest route, to get something done as quickly as possible.	Consider and evaluate other ways of responding.

Our worldview shapes how we form core beliefs about ourselves, others, the world and our spirituality. Our worldview is shaped by:

- our culture
- our childhood relationships
- the historical events that have shaped our lives, our parents'/carers' lives and previous generations' lives
- the ethical and spiritual values and beliefs that we choose to live by.

Our core beliefs shape our automatic thoughts. Taking time to consider our core beliefs and how they influence our lives is a valuable step towards understanding ourselves. Awareness of our thoughts and beliefs, combined with compassion and curiosity, provides the foundation for the formation of a thought life and beliefs that encourage wellbeing.

Examples to nurture wellbeing in our thinking life

Thought, thinking distortions and related emotions	Compassionate alternatives to the thinking distortion and related emotion	What can I do to be compassionate to myself and others?
For example: **Thought:** "No one will speak to me at the party as they think I'm boring." **Thinking distortions:** Catastrophising Globalising Mind-reading Negative focus **Related emotions:** Anxiety	"I have been friends with Tom (the party host) for a year and we share fun conversations." "It is normal at a party that some people will be more extrovert and chatty and some more shy, like me. Just because I take a while to feel at ease with new people doesn't mean I am boring." "I have no evidence that the other guests will think I'm boring as they haven't met me yet." "Everyone knows the party host in some way so I could begin a conversation with 'How do you know Tom?' and ask about their life." **Related emotions:** I am feeling a little nervous, however also looking forward to seeing Tom and curious to meet his other friends.	I will remind myself of the compassionate alternative thoughts on the journey to the party and during the party. If I feel anxious on the journey I will do my relaxation breathing. I will remind myself that we are all different and that it is OK to be shyer than others. If I see another guest on their own, I will introduce myself and ask, "How do you know Tom?" I can ask Tom if there is anything I can do to help with the party.

Sam and thinking wellbeing

In chapter three we saw how Sam's feelings of anxiety had led to anxious thoughts, impeding his ability to think clearly and to problem solve. Sam telling himself "Don't be silly" hints that his thinking was becoming judgemental towards himself. We can see how Sam's thinking had moved into the hyper-arousal zone with repressed childhood memories of his parents' arguments over money intruding into his thought life.

Sam's supervisor's enquiry, "How would you like to respond?" enabled Sam to draw from the Wellbeing Zone's PEACE model and "enquire" and "ask" questions of himself. By reading the Wellbeing Zone's table of common thinking distortions, Sam recognised that he was personalising his family's finances. This then led to the "creativity" of his response. Instead of feeling the burden of his family finances resting solely on him, suggesting a possible personalising thinking distortion, Sam was able to step back from his thoughts, recognise the thinking distortion and then challenge it with the more compassionate and realistic statement of "It's understandable why someone with my background may have these immediate thoughts and feelings." We see here how Sam's worldview and his life experiences influenced his thinking. Sam then "engaged" or took action by having a collaborative and creative discussion with his spouse, where they were able to discern a new pathway forward for them in relation to family finances.

Chapter 9

Behavioural wellbeing

Behavioural life		
HYPER-AROUSAL ZONE Fight-or-flight response	**WELLBEING ZONE** Befriending response	**HYPO-AROUSAL ZONE** Freeze-or-fold response
Becoming increasingly obsessive, repetitive, impulsive, hostile, on edge or hyper-vigilant; vulnerable to numbing, spacing-out or addictions.	Attuned to the present moment; responses adapting to the situation to enable the wellbeing and flourishing of self, others and creation; consideration of the past, present and future; courageous; taking initiative; being able to delay gratification; ability to play; creativity.	Becoming passive, withdrawn, isolating and shutdown; drawn towards numbing, spacing-out or addictions; operating on autopilot.

The ability to adapt behaviour according to life's challenges and difficulties, taking into consideration the wellbeing of ourselves, others and nature, is key for flourishing. In the hyper- and hypo-arousal zones, our behaviours can be drawn towards automatic survival responses. These automatic behaviours:

- are drawn towards a focus on self for survival
- are often unconscious, so we are not aware of what is driving our behaviour
- provide immediate comfort, sense of relief, or avoid emotions and things we find uncomfortable. These are sometimes called numbing, spacing out or avoidant behaviours
- may have become ingrained patterns of behaviour, a habit or addiction that is hard to change.

We will all at some time have found ourselves behaving automatically. While automatic survival responses enable us to survive to the best of our ability in times of difficulty or trauma, we can find that when life has changed they are no longer serving us well. An example would be avoiding sharing information that might be perceived as vulnerable with others because that served us well when others betrayed our trust previously. However, if we are now in a safe, trusting relationship, avoidance of emotional intimacy can impede the flourishing of the depth of the relationship.

Learning new skills that enable a change in behaviour requires courage and takes time (often a considerable amount). We can probably all relate to making one or two tentative steps forwards and then experiencing a step or two backwards when we've tried to make a change. Patterns of behaviour create neural pathways in the brain so that the behaviour becomes an automatic response. It takes time to create new neural pathways. Compassion, curiosity and creativity are key. Curiosity enables a "let's try this and see what happens" approach and therefore avoids a "success/fail" perspective, which can impede the creativity required for sustained behavioural changes.

The ABC behavioural model is a CBT intervention that is used in understanding behaviour and is also used widely in educational settings and parenting resources.[48,49]

- **A**ctivating event – the details of what happened beforehand.
- **B**eliefs – beliefs about the event (our thinking life).
- **C**onsequences – how our emotional and behavioural life has been impacted.

The ABC mnemonic offers a simple stepped model for understanding the contributing factors that have influenced why we have opted to behave in certain ways. This is helpful to unpack when we want to change behaviours that are not serving us or others well. Examining the red and blue areas of the table above, take time to notice the details of behaviours that you want to understand better in order to make different choices. Expanding on the ABC model:

- What is/was the activating event, the beliefs and the emotional and behavioural consequences (the ABC model)?

- Do these patterns of behaviour occur in only some life areas and not in others (e.g. in the workplace but not in close relationships or friendships)?

- Are there any external contributing factors (e.g. organisational expectations of how to respond)?

- How does this behaviour impact on others and myself (e.g. are colleagues impacted by my aggressive behaviour? Do I like myself when my behaviour is aggressive?)

This provides information to then consider what may be helpful interventions to enable a change in behaviour towards wellbeing.

As patterns of behaviour are formed from neural pathways, it can take time to change. It can help to:

- take a stepped approach by breaking the change of behaviour into smaller steps that feel manageable and reviewing after each step. If a step hasn't worked out as hoped, view this as useful information to gain insight and learning from, to enable the next step to be created

- start something new to replace an unhelpful habit, for example eating fruit or vegetable snacks between meals rather than trying to stop eating sweets

- celebrate doing the new behaviour rather than waiting to celebrate when we have achieved the goal (but when we do achieve the goal, celebrate too)

- focus on the positives and how this is experienced within our different life areas – this creates memories of helpful change

- consider wider influences and ask: what enables flourishing?

- include others for accountability, encouragement and the sharing of ideas to support wellbeing. Support of others is particularly helpful when we are struggling with a behaviour that has become an addictive pattern.

Addictions arise because we initially found the behaviour pleasant; it provided comfort, a thrill or an escape from emotional distress and stress. Often this is an unconscious response. When we are struggling with an addiction, seeking specialist help can help support the changes we desire to make for our wellbeing, and for those impacted by our addictive behaviour.

Sam and behavioural wellbeing

A month after Sam had stepped back to working on alternate Saturdays as a taxi driver, he reviewed his wellbeing using the Wellbeing Zone table and the Wellbeing Zone's PEACE model. Before his changes to working at weekends, he had been moving towards the hypo-arousal zone in his physical life, hyper-arousal zone with his emotional, thinking, behavioural and relational life, and swinging between the hyper- and hypo-arousal zones in his spiritual life. Sam noticed he was now in the green-coloured wellbeing zone for the six different life areas. Sam's life was full with a role he enjoyed and found rewarding, but it was also demanding, and he knew the decisions that he needed to make as a consequence of the freeze in funding would be difficult. He was aware of how demanding the roles were for his team too and worked hard to support and develop the whole team. He also had a busy home life with teenage children.

Sam found the Wellbeing Zone table and the Wellbeing Zone's PEACE model provided a helpful structure to enable him to step back and consider his wellbeing. He found having printed copies helpful, and had them taped into his journal. He liked to make himself a cup of his favourite coffee and sit down for 10–15 minutes and read them and write what he noticed about himself so he could look back and see any changes that had been made. He also found it helpful to write down any questions or ideas he wanted to mull over.

Sam was aware that his nature was to leap towards immediately fixing problems, both his own and for others, and that he often overlooked the impact that his immediate fixing behaviours were having on himself and on others. He was aware this probably stemmed from his childhood; being the oldest child, and a son, he had tried to help his mum when his dad left. He could see that was what had driven his decision to work every weekend as a taxi driver. As Sam thought about the "ask" section in the PEACE model, thinking about what the deeper needs behind his behaviour of jumping in to quickly fix problems might be, he became aware of the inner pain he had repressed when his dad left. At the time, he didn't have the emotional language and insight to understand and express what he felt. As a boy, he delighted in the status of being "Mum's superman", a game his mum had created to get her children helping with household chores. Sam was always first to finish his allocated chores and receive a big hug from his mum.

Sam was grateful for his spouse, who had been keen to discuss the impact of him working every weekend. Sam hadn't realised the effect it was having on the rest of the family, as they were missing family time together. As Sam reviewed the family finances and the patterns of work for him and his spouse and considered each person's wellbeing by matching what he noticed in each person with the Wellbeing Zone's descriptions, he could sense it would be helpful to consider a few adjustments. He planned to discuss his observations and ideas with his spouse.

Can you see how Sam's pattern of behaviour of immediately fixing problems evolved? It served him, and his mum, well in his childhood, but now it was placing him at risk of burnout and hindering his current family relationships. What do you think Sam's core belief may be? It could possibly be: "To be loved I need to fix others' problems." Sam shared with his spouse what he noticed about himself and others in the family, and included his spouse and teenage children in thinking through a plan to cultivate wellbeing for all the individuals in the family as well as the family as a whole. By considering the wider influences to his behaviour and inviting his family to share ideas and support him, Sam was creating accountability and encouragement to assist him and his family.

In this chapter we have focused on Sam; the next chapter will be centred around Dani and her relational life.

Chapter 10
Relational wellbeing

Relational life		
HYPER-AROUSAL ZONE Fight-or-flight response	**WELLBEING ZONE** Befriending response	**HYPO-AROUSAL ZONE** Freeze-or-fold response
Becoming increasingly over-reactive, agitated, defensive, avoiding, dominating, demanding, critical, intolerant, exploitative, abusive, self-absorbed or anxious towards others; inclination towards compulsive caretaking or controlling of others; disregarding relational boundaries.	Attunement to and proactive in the development of relationships where all can flourish; sense of relational peace; awareness of and maintenance of healthy relational boundaries; being able to form inter-dependent relationships that are collaborative, accountable and respectful with intimacy and commitment; being humble, tolerant, honest and genuine.	Becoming avoidant, detached, ambivalent, rejecting or dependent in relationships; self-absorbed; vulnerable to others control, neglect or abuse; losing ability to defend self, initiate responsibility and care of self and others; vulnerability to be unable to maintain healthy boundaries; tendency to be critical of others; struggle to receive affirmation; vulnerability to dissociate from reality.

Relational wellbeing is dependent on our ongoing attention to our relationships with ourselves, with others, with nature and with our spirituality so that we may live in *shalom*, or relational peace. The Wellbeing Zone draws on neuro-biological developmental attachment theories, alongside the relational qualities that are known to support the development of relational flourishing.

At birth, we as babies are totally dependent on our carers to meet our needs. How our caregivers (those who cared for us when we were growing up) responded to our needs for relational, emotional and physical comfort shape our developing brain in how we then relate to others. The British psychiatrist John Bowlby and the American-Canadian psychologist Mary Ainsworth's research into the relationships between children and their carers in the 1960s and 1970s identified four distinct attachment styles or patterns. Their work is known as Attachment Theory.[50]

Attachment patterns

Attachment pattern	Child's experience of carer	Child's pattern of relating which continues into adulthood
Secure	Carer is compassionately attuned and attentive to the child's needs.	Able to form secure, compassionate relationships with others. Able to collaboratively trust and depend on others.
Avoidant	Carer is not attuned and attentive to the child's emotional and relational needs.	Uncomfortable or fearful of intimacy, emotionally unavailable. Prefers to be independent and self-reliant. Struggles to compromise.
Anxious	Carer is inconsistent, alternating between being attuned and then not being attuned to the child's needs. The child doesn't know what to expect.	Feels insecure in relationships, craves intimacy but fearful others will abandon them. Intimacy can feel overwhelming. Hungry for validation.
Disorganised	Carer consistently fails to respond compassionately to child's needs. Carer fails to meet the appropriate developmental needs of a child.	Deep desire for closeness to others coupled with a tendency to avoid or push others away. Fear response to intimacy. Behaviour can be inconsistent due to being triggered by past painful relational experiences. Can feel deeply unsafe when in relationships with others.

Disorganised attachment is sometimes called "trauma bonding" as this pattern can arise from experiences of abusive relationships.

Attachment patterns are a survival response to the relationships we experienced in childhood. While a main attachment pattern may predominate in our relationships with others, different relationships can move us towards a different attachment style.[51,52] Culture impacts how prevalent a particular attachment style may be. Within each attachment pattern there will be a wide difference in the features of how each person may relate. Attachment patterns can be changed by relationships. This can provide healing when we have formed a trauma bonding attachment pattern or an anxious or avoidant attachment pattern.

Relational boundaries which respect that each person has a unique identity and individual infinite worth provide the potential for relational wellbeing. Like attachment patterns, relational boundaries are learned from our childhood experiences of our relationships with our carers. Healthy relational boundaries occur when individuals in the relationship can find a balance and harmony between relational engagement and autonomy to enable wellbeing for all. For children, autonomy needs to be age-appropriate so that they are safe. Maintaining healthy relational boundaries requires collaboration, accountability, respect, commitment and appropriate intimacy. This enables healthy inter-dependent relationships to flourish. The relational qualities of being compassionately humble, tolerant, honest and genuine all help relational wellbeing to flourish.

"Othering" is when a person or group is consciously or unconsciously generalised for their differences and these differences are seen as a threat or looked down upon.[53] Othering creates an environment for discrimination, disregarding, blaming, projecting and abuse to arise. Othering disregards the innate infinite worth of each person and is the root of much relational conflict and abuse. Trauma can create relational experiences of being othered, which is traumatic and evokes our innate survival responses. For those who have not experienced being othered due to an innate aspect of who we are, it can be hard to comprehend the magnitude of trauma caused by othering.

The opposite of "othering" can be termed "withing".[54] "Withing" describes qualities of relating where separate identities are honoured, coupled with compassion and care. Withing enables relationships that have secure attachment qualities of relating. In the Gospels, although the actual words "withing" and "othering" are not specifically used, Jesus is described as having "withing" qualities in the way he related to others who had been "othered" by society. The Gospels are full of stories describing how Jesus related to others who were being marginalised or mistreated. For example, Jesus touched a man with leprosy, bringing not only physical healing but also relational inclusion back into society in an era when people with leprosy were ostracised (Luke 5:12-14). Jesus engaged in conversation with a Samaritan woman at a well too (John 4:4-26). Culturally at that time, men did not talk to women in public, and, on top of that, Jews despised Samaritans. Although Jesus is considered both human and divine by Christians, the Gospels reveal Jesus relating in a collaborative, interdependent way with his disciples. How Jesus related to others enabled relational inclusion and belonging, care, healing and renewed collaborative relationships. These are all features of *shalom*, or wellbeing.

Businesswoman and counsellor Sharon McLean has developed a simple practical cultural model to cultivate relationships with "withing" qualities. The McLean ABC Cultural Competence Model's focus is on incorporating inclusion and diversity into a cultural context and being committed to hospitality for all.[55] The model describes an ongoing circular experience of:

- **A**cceptance: valuing each person's cultural background and experience, seeking to understand their worldview

- **B**elonging: valuing, hearing and enabling each person's perspective to contribute to an endeavour

- **C**ommitment: to continually learn and change to enable cultural inclusion and celebration of diversity.

Dani, Jo and relational wellbeing

In chapter one we learned that Dani's family life was shattered by the outbreak of war and then she was trafficked into modern slavery. Back home, Dani had either known or recognised most of the people she saw day to day. She'd grown up in a culture where men and boys had different roles compared to the women and girls. Although she didn't voice her feelings, she knew that she was treated differently from her brothers, and sensed she mattered less. Dani didn't have the freedom to make decisions. With the women in her family, she was able to chat freely, but with the men she said very little.

When Dani was initially taken from her home, the older woman who oversaw the people doing domestic work in the house she was taken to was harsh with Dani and made her work long hours. However, this woman also offered kindness to Dani at times. Dani never knew how the woman would respond to her and so was always on edge. She tried to please the woman, as Dani's wellbeing was reliant on the woman's changing whims. The woman told Dani she was lucky as her hard work had earned her the opportunity to go to the UK and work in the woman's friend's home. She was told she would earn good money to repay her family debts quicker. The journey to the UK took weeks. Dani never knew what was happening and was continually frightened.

Considering attachment styles, in childhood Dani may have formed a secure attachment style with her mother and the women in her family, and perhaps an avoidant attachment style with her father and the men in the family. We can see she experienced a disorganised attachment or trauma bonding from the woman and traffickers; she depended on them for her safety and wellbeing, but they were unpredictable, unkind and abusive. Her boundaries were disregarded, exploited and abused. Understanding Dani's past attachment experiences gives insight into why she was wary of Sam and Jo to begin with, and shared very little about herself. This was a healthy survival response, and it was important for her to take time to trust people she didn't know, especially because she had experienced abusive relationships.

While Dani was wary of Sam and Jo, she was quietly observing them and the other people at the centre. Each time she went to the centre, she found Jo and the other staff consistent and respectful and when they said they would do something, they did it. They seemed honest and committed to the welfare of the other clients. If they couldn't do something, they explained why. The staff at the centre reflected the cultural diversity of the local community. Dani felt valued and welcomed by their interest in her culture. She felt Jo genuinely sought to understand both her culture and her personally. Jo took time to explain things and checked with Dani that she understood, and Dani was respected and allowed to make her own decisions. Dani found this daunting at first but, through Jo's support, Dani began to feel able to make choices that contributed towards her wellbeing.

Jo had explained how Dani could contact her during the hours when she would be available. Dani often felt frightened in the evenings in her room and asked Jo if it was possible to chat over the telephone during these "out of hours" times. Jo was compassionately empathic to Dani's feelings of fear by conveying her care and insight into Dani's situation. Jo explained her working hours to Dani and introduced her to a couple of organisations that provided supportive listening care in the evenings. Several of the other clients shared with Dani that they had found these helpful too. Jo and Dani used the Wellbeing Zone's PEACE model to think of ways Dani could care for herself when she felt alone or frightened.

Dani could see how hard Jo worked. Some of the other clients could be upset and demanding at times, but Jo remained patient, talking in a clear, kind voice, and clearly relaying the boundaries of what she was able to do.

Dani found the Wellbeing Zone's PEACE model helped her develop the ability to think about each of the problems she faced and how she may make a step forward to foster her wellbeing. At first, she found the creative section hard as she couldn't think what she might do. Gradually, by listening to others, and through her conversations with Jo, Dani began to think of small ways she could help nurture her own wellbeing. Dani found the care and respect shown to her by Jo and the other staff at the centre enabled her to grow in care and respect of herself.

While Dani was trying hard to get into a daily pattern of going to bed at the same time to help improve her sleep, a friend she had made at the centre asked her to chat late at night. Dani was aware she wanted to help her friend, but also knew her health would improve if she maintained a regular earlier bedtime. By following Jo's example of making clear her care for her friend, sharing the resources and things she had found helpful to soothe her anxious feelings, explaining why she had a set bedtime and letting her friend know when she was free to chat, Dani was able to care for herself and her friend through her compassionate boundaries. Initially, she felt guilty for stating her boundaries. She discussed this with Jo the next day. Jo invited her to share what other emotions she might be feeling too. Dani found this hard, so Jo gave her a copy of Wellbeing Zone's wheel of emotions to look at to see if she recognised any of the other emotions within herself. Dani noticed she had also felt vulnerable, courageous and restless the day before. Dani talked with Jo about what may lie behind her different feelings. Jo shared her experiences of putting boundaries in place around her working hours. Dani began to see that by putting boundaries in place that supported her wellbeing, alongside thoughtful care for others, she too could nurture her wellbeing and show her care for others. Her friend had found Dani's help and modelling of healthy boundaries helpful and had decided to develop healthier sleep patterns herself too.

Chapter 11
Spiritual wellbeing

Spiritual life		
HYPER-AROUSAL ZONE Fight-or-flight response	**WELLBEING ZONE** Befriending response	**HYPO-AROUSAL ZONE** Freeze-or-fold response
Losing the capacity to form and connect with core beliefs, values and sustaining practices that recognise self and others hold infinite worth and care for nature; losing sense of peace, joy and mystery; becoming entitled, impatient and exploitative; struggling to give and receive forgiveness; losing ability to enjoy beauty and sense of awe and wonder; at risk of radicalisation.	Having the capacity to form and connect with core beliefs, values and sustaining practices during suffering and everyday life that recognise self and others hold infinite worth and care of nature; nurturing peace and wellbeing for self and all; giving and receiving forgiveness; accepting mystery; seeking justice for all; holding qualities of hope, compassion, patience, gratitude, generosity and kindness; enjoying beauty and sense of awe and wonder. Altruism.	Losing the capacity to form and connect with core beliefs, values and sustaining practices that recognise self and others hold infinite worth and care for nature; increasing compassion fatigue in care of self, others and creation; becoming bitter; vulnerable to injustice and moral injury; struggling to give and receive forgiveness; sensing emptiness, hopelessness, despair and life is meaningless; struggling to notice and enjoy beauty; losing sense of awe and wonder.

The Wellbeing Zone table describes spiritual features that research has identified as helpful in contributing to wellbeing not only for our spiritual life, but also in our other areas of life. These elements are: giving and receiving forgiveness; accepting mystery; seeking justice for all; holding qualities of hope, compassion, patience, gratitude, generosity and kindness; enjoying beauty and a sense of awe and wonder; and altruism. We have already looked at compassion and gratitude in chapter seven, and in chapter four we looked at some descriptions of what may be helpful to consider when we think about spiritual wellbeing. This included the invitation to see human spirituality as living in *shalom* in our relationship with ourselves, with others, with nature and with the transcendental (relating to something or someone beyond the human level). For a Christian, this would be relating with the person of God as described in the Bible.

In chapter five we looked at the five facets of post-traumatic growth: a deeper appreciation of life; warmer and more intimate relationships; a better sense of who we are and our personal strengths; awareness of new possibilities in life; and positive spiritual growth. We discussed that trauma intrinsically challenges our core beliefs about ourselves, about others, about the world and about the existence, character and nature of God. It is our questioning, our search to form satisfactory answers to the deep questions that trauma evokes, that lays the pathway towards spiritual growth.

Flourishing, seeking justice and altruism

Rowan Williams, a former Anglican archbishop, discusses that human flourishing is dependent on a number of human challenges: how we individually respond to our innate dependence on others and personal autonomy; passion that resides in each one of us to foster wellbeing; use of time that enables a purposeful, meaningful life and our ability to accept our human mortality.[56]

Our spirituality shapes how we navigate these four human challenges. The Wellbeing Zone's spiritual zone begins with a description of spiritual wellbeing as "having the capacity to form and connect with core beliefs, values and sustaining practices during suffering and everyday life that recognise self and others hold infinite worth and care of nature; nurturing peace and wellbeing for self and all". These qualities reflect the spirituality of Jesus when he lived on earth and how his relationship with God the Father and the Holy Spirit enabled him to touch others with God's gift of *shalom* both in day-to-day life and when experiencing profound suffering. The Gospel stories also reveal how Jesus chose to live in relation to the four things described by Williams that support human flourishing.

It is clear from the Gospel stories that Jesus chose a life of altruism – a selfless concern for others' wellbeing – which many times brought personal suffering. Jesus' life was also one of seeking justice, a genuine care for the wellbeing for all people, for both our life lived on earth and for our eternal wellbeing. When Jesus was asked what the most important instruction for living well is, Jesus replied: "Love the Lord your God with all your heart and with all your soul and with all your mind and with all your strength . . . Love your neighbour as yourself" (Mark 12:30-31, NIVUK, also in Matthew 22:37-39, Luke 10:27).

Jesus' actions weren't those of people pleasing, seeking immediate or short-term comfort at the expense of lasting wellbeing. At times, Jesus challenged or disrupted others' privilege or comfort with the purpose of enabling lasting *shalom* or wellbeing aligned to God's values for not only the individuals concerned, but also for others. An example of this was when Jesus drove out the stallholders who were selling at the temple, as this was exploitative and impeded the prayer life of those worshipping at the temple (Luke 19:45-46). Jesus also invited his disciples "to carry their cross and follow me" (Luke 14:27, NIVUK). Both the pursuit of seeking justice for all and the pursuit of altruism often lead us out of our wellbeing zone across many areas of our life. For example, physical tiredness due to the demands of giving out to others or emotional distress from caring for others who are suffering.

The Wellbeing Zone seeks to invite compassionate awareness of how the choice to be altruistic or seek justice can impact wellbeing, so decisions are considered wisely and thought is given to enable sustainable actions that bear fruit. It is important when looking at Jesus as the ultimate role model to remember that Jesus was both fully human and fully divine when he lived on earth: "who being in the very nature God . . . taking the very nature of a servant, being made in human likeness" (Philippians 2:6-8, NIVUK). Christians understand that Jesus, being divine, had the wisdom that we as humans don't fully have. Christians believe that while humanity may have the image of God within each person, we are not divine. We and others are not perfect. We all have our personal strengths, things we find more of a challenge and things we are unable to do but others can. Remembering our humanity allows us to be compassionate to ourselves and compassionate to others when we struggle despite our best intentions and efforts.

Accepting mystery and wellbeing

James Fowler, an American psychologist and theologian, created a model from extensive research describing the stages of development in our spiritual life.[57] His research identified that spiritual wellbeing and maturity includes the belief that life innately holds mystery. In chapter three we saw that Job's wrestling with the question of why he was suffering enabled him to conclude: "Do you think you can explain the mystery of God . . . God is far higher than you can imagine, far deeper than you can comprehend" (Job 11:7-12, *The Message*). In science and art, mystery creates a juncture; gaps in knowledge are an important driver for curiosity and creativity, leading to advances and innovations, while an acceptance of mystery can stifle growth and development, ultimately impeding wellbeing.[58] The "Serenity Prayer",[59] which is interwoven into the resources Alcoholics Anonymous offers, captures the wisdom of discerning when the acceptance of mystery is helpful for wellbeing and when it is not.

> God grant me the serenity
> To accept the things I cannot change,
> Courage to change the things I can;
> And the wisdom to know the difference.

Suffering and wellbeing

Seeking to understand the root causes of suffering is key for providing an explanation of why something has happened. It allows valuable learning, including about how to prevent further suffering. While answers to these questions are immensely valuable, they don't necessarily get to the heart of the magnitude of the questions that suffering arouses. The late American theologian and pastor Tim Keller offered a description of the role of mystery within suffering: "to trust God when we do not understand God, is to treat God as God and not another human being".[60] The transcendence (outside of humanity's full comprehension) and immanence (knowable) nature of God within Christianity stirs many questions, including aspects of mystery. The story of Jesus in the garden of Gethsemane (Matthew 26:36-46, Luke 22:39-46) describes Jesus in anguish at the suffering that lay ahead of him with his imminent arrest and crucifixion. Twice in the garden of Gethsemane Jesus prayed "may your [God's] will be done" (NIVUK). The Gospel of John also describes Jesus' wrestling with his impending death. "Now my soul is troubled, and what shall I say? 'Father, save me from this hour'? No, it was for this very reason I came to this hour. Father, glorify your name" (John 12:27-28, NIVUK). Jesus found wisdom and spiritual peace amid unimaginable trauma and suffering through the choice to allow God to be glorified through him, through his trust in God. The British Anglican Dean Philip Plyming explains that discerning how we might glorify God amid suffering can provide a pathway in such times that compassionately cares for ourselves and others and honestly reveals "the God of Good Friday and Easter Sunday . . . the story of the crucified and resurrected Jesus".[61] Christians have the gift of knowing God's presence in suffering and the gift of hope in the promises of God.

Recognising, responding to and preventing spiritual abuse

Spiritual beliefs and practices can become othering, disregarding, exploitative or abusive towards others when a person's spiritual life moves into the hyper- or hypo-arousal zones. Religious intolerance and persecution of others holding different beliefs and practices, both within the same religion or across different religions, has caused and continues to cause much suffering globally.

While religious intolerance and persecution is often overt – the systematic oppression and ill-treatment of others who hold different, and often minority, religious beliefs or affiliations – spiritual abuse can be harder to recognise. Spiritual abuse is a form of psychological or emotional abuse characterised by coercive or controlling behaviour within a religious context. The impact of spiritual abuse can be far reaching, harming a person's relationship with themselves, with others and with God.

Recent reports into spiritual abuse within UK Christian organisations have identified the need for awareness and learning within Christian communities of what the features of safe, healthy relationships and spirituality where all can flourish are, and what the features of abusive relationships are.[62] These reports also highlight the usefulness of safe, respectful, collaborative reflective practices within religious organisations so that abusive behaviour can be identified swiftly, safeguarding practices and procedures can be implemented, and the harm can be acknowledged and addressed. These findings echo recent research on spiritual abuse and initiatives that create safe, healthy spiritual communities.[63,64,65]

The Wellbeing Zone seeks to offer an awareness of the features of healthy relationships and a spiritual life so that potential abusive ways of relating can be promptly identified and appropriate welfare responses put in place.

Moral injury

You will see in the Wellbeing Zone's spiritual life hypo-arousal zone the phrase "vulnerable to injustice and moral injury". While a moral injury can occur regardless of which spiritual zone we personally are in, the impact of a moral injury often has the features described in the Wellbeing Zone's hypo- and hyper-arousal zones. The term "moral injury" was first applied in the military and has become helpful for understanding the emotional, thinking, relational and spiritual responses that can occur when a person witnesses, perpetrates or fails to prevent acts that violate their personal, moral and ethical values and expectations of themselves.[66] Healthcare professionals, relief and charity workers and those responding to crisis or disaster situations can also experience a moral injury when the resources available are unable to meet the needs of people suffering.[67]

Moral and ethical values are the values a person chooses to live by. They may include, for example, values of fairness, accountability, courage and the avoidance of harm to others. These values can be shaped by a person's religion and culture. They can be assumed or be a thoughtfully considered personal set of values to live by. Our values can change over our lifetime, too. A life-changing event may prompt a re-evaluation of life values. Features of moral injury may include guilt and shame due to expectations of self and others. Such injury can arise from others' superhuman expectations, or unrealistic heroic expectations of oneself that don't take into account natural human limitations and vulnerabilities.

Research has shown inviting the person to describe what a "loving, forgiving and compassionate moral authority" would say to them allows a compassionate realistic understanding of the situation and their actions when a moral injury has occurred.[68] While these characteristics of a moral authority are compatible with a Christian understanding of God, it is important when addressing spirituality within therapeutic endeavours that sensitivity towards and respect of a person's religion and unique spiritualty is upheld, as spirituality is comprised of deeply personal and sensitive beliefs. The Churchill Framework provides guidance on ethical considerations in relation to responding thoughtfully to a person's unique spirituality.[69]

Grieving

Recognising suffering includes recognising what has been lost through the suffering. Learning how to grieve well, whether our loss is from a bereavement, a loss of a relationship, job, health, opportunity or expectation, provides a pathway for healing and living with the extent of the loss. The Dual Process model of grief offers a holistic understanding to grieving.[70] Healthy grieving requires that we honestly face the loss and what the loss means for us and for others, including recognising and attending to the emotional pain. Anger and sadness are natural emotions in grieving. Both take time, energy and wisdom to attend to well. Healthy grieving also requires that we compassionately attend to our ongoing daily life, even though this can be hard after a significant bereavement. Grieving healthily means that we will move between these two undertakings: compassionately attending to our emotional life and the things we need to do in everyday living. Grieving enables us to keep living well in the face of loss.[71]

Forgiveness

Forgiveness is central to Christianity. Jesus encouraged his followers to pray: "Keep us forgiven with you and forgiving others" (Matthew 6:12, *The Message*). Christians believe that God will forgive someone when they repent for their actions that have caused harm. In chapter four we looked at the Hebrew word *"Teshuva"*, which includes in its meaning "to return", "to change", "a transformation", and the idea that to repent is to return to a compassionate God to receive a new beginning.

Forgiveness is not limited to religious contexts. Psychologically, the act of forgiving has been shown to enable the release of anger or resentment when we have been hurt by others.[72] Without the act of forgiveness, we risk becoming entangled emotionally in the injustice or the harmful impact of a person's actions, impeding our wellbeing and ability to move forwards with our life.

Forgiveness is not something that can be demanded. It does not negate the harm caused, nor does it mean reconciliation or a return to how life used to be. It also does not mean that the offence should go unpunished. Forgiveness can be more difficult when the offender does not acknowledge the offence, is insincere or avoids or deflects true responsibility for their actions. However, forgiveness has been shown to bring wellbeing to the person who is doing the forgiving, whether we are forgiving ourselves or others – and whether the other person acknowledges their wrongdoing or not.

Forgiveness can be a challenging process that can take time. It does not require the offender to be present; when abuse has occurred, the victim's safety is paramount. A stepped approach to forgiveness provides a supportive structure by understanding each stage of the process of forgiving. This includes the recognition of the facts as well as allowing the processing of painful emotions.[73,74] Stepped forgiveness approaches can include:

- an honest recognition of the suffering caused, either by us or by others to us

- respectful sensitivity to the victim's welfare

- an honest placing of responsibility for what has happened on the person(s) who actually caused the harm

- understanding how the perpetrator's guilt and shame may have unknowingly spread to the victim. An honest recognition of where blame lies lays the pathway towards freedom from false guilt and shame

- acknowledging and processing the painful emotions

- for the offender, acknowledging and processing guilt and remorse. This lays the base for an honest apology and a commitment to compassionately change the offending behaviour

- restoration. For the offender to make amends if this is possible and in the victim's best interests

- a recognition that forgiveness may provide the starting point towards reconciliation. However, the victim's safety and wellbeing are paramount. In some circumstances, it may not be wise or in the victim's best interests to have contact with an offender

- renewal, which means choosing to learn from the experience and seek actions where wellbeing and flourishing can grow.

Hope

Grief can bring up feelings of hopelessness as we have lost someone or something dear to us. Within the Wellbeing Zone table, you may have noticed that hope is placed in both the emotional and spiritual areas of life. This is because hope is an emotion and a belief. While these two aspects are interrelated, distinguishing between the emotion and the belief can bring helpful insight. Christianity offers many promises, or hopes, in God's nature and provision:

"We have this hope as an anchor for the soul, firm and secure" (Hebrews 6:19, NIVUK). A Christian may know the hope of God's promises for them (a belief), but emotionally feel a loss of hope due to the reality of a situation where expectations are fading or lost.

In chapter seven we discussed that emotions give us insight into ourselves and how we are experiencing life at a given moment. At times, feeling and finding hope can be a struggle. Noticing shifts in the emotion of hope can provide awareness of our current situation and discernment of what may be the best pathway forwards. This may include grieving and lamenting for lost hopes or re-adjusting goals and actions in light of current circumstances.

Loss of hope is a significant risk factor for suicidal thoughts and behaviours. It can be hard to know what to say, both for the person wrestling with the suicidal thoughts and for those around them. If we are aware that we, or someone else, are struggling with suicidal thoughts, getting support and help is key. However alone we may feel, taking the step to talk to someone enables the supportive care we need at these times of distress to be put in place. In the UK, the NHS, the Samaritans and many other organisations provide specialist support and care for when we're struggling with our mental health.[75]

Finding, building and strengthening hope includes exploring things outside ourselves that may nurture hope as well as drawing on our inner resources.[76] "To hope" involves discerning who and what is wise to trust in.

The psychologist Erik Erikson developed his psychosocial stages of development model to depict how the virtues or qualities of growth and maturity arise out of successfully grappling with opposing tensions. Opposing tensions bring up core spiritual or existential questions about who we are. Each stage lays the foundation for the next stage to be developed. While Erikson's model has a framework based on biological age ranges, the premise is that these opposing tensions form a continuum that may re-surface and be resolved at later stages in our lifespan. For example, if a pre-school child is criticised by their carers when they struggle to learn new things, the virtue of "purpose" may not fully evolve, and so the child will be reluctant to take initiative. However, if when they start school they have an attentive, encouraging teacher who praises the child for trying new things, the child will begin to learn that it is safe and rewarding to take initiative. The virtue of purpose will begin to grow in the child.

The first stage in Erikson's model is the question: "Can I trust that my needs will be met?" with the consequent virtue of hope. The infant acquires the virtue of hope through their caregivers consistently and lovingly providing for their welfare developmental needs. Erikson's model highlights the foundational importance of hope in human flourishing.

Erikson's psychosocial stages of development model[77]

Stage	Basic conflict and major question	Virtue	Description
Infancy	Trust vs mistrust. "Can I trust the world?"	Hope	Trust that needs will be met.
Early childhood	Autonomy vs shame/doubt. "When can I do things myself and when do I rely on others?"	Will	Develop a sense of ability to make choices.
Pre-early school age	Initiative vs guilt. "Is it OK for me to do things?"	Purpose	Develop ability to take initiative.
School age	Industry vs inferiority. "How can I be good?"	Competence	Develop self-confidence in abilities when competent or unconfident when not.
Adolescence	Identity vs confusion. "Who am I?"	Fidelity (secure sense of self)	Experiment with and develop identity and roles.
Early adulthood	Intimacy vs isolation. "Can I love and be loved?"	Love	Establish intimacy and relationships with others.
Middle age	Generativity vs stagnation. "What can I contribute to the world?"	Care	Contribute to society and be part of a family.
Older age	Integrity vs despair. "How was my life a good life?"	Wisdom	Assess and make sense of life and meaning of contribution to the world and others.

The virtues described in Erikson's model are also virtues that are attributed to spiritual wellbeing and flourishing. Erikson's model describes spiritual growth happening throughout our lives if we choose to wrestle with the opposing tensions and existential questions that each life stage presents us with.

The Canadian psychologist and Christian spiritual director David Benner has created a model of existential questions that correlate with the different aspects of human development.[78] These are questions that are relevant to each season or age in life and can foster spiritual enquiry and growth.

Benner's model of dimensions of development and existential questions

Dimensions of development	Existential questions
Self	Who am I?
Values	What is important to me?
Moral	How should I choose?
Interpersonal	How should I relate to others?
Spiritual	What is of ultimate concern?
Needs	What do I need to be well?
Kinesthetic	How do I indwell my body?
Emotional	How do I feel?
Aesthetic	What do I find attractive?
Cognitive	What am I aware of?
Ego	How do I wish to appear?
Faith	Whom and how do I trust?

Growth and maturity take time to develop. Patience is the ability to accept that hope can take time to come to fruition, but that it is worth continuing to be proactive in working towards a desired hope. When we are exploring deep questions about ourselves and about our spirituality, we will often be confronted with paradoxes. Christianity visibly contains many paradoxes. We have talked about God being a compassionate God in Christianity, but we have also talked about injustice, suffering, grieving, moral injury and forgiveness. Wrestling with paradoxes can become a place of compassionate spiritual growth.[79] Patience enables us to compassionately endure difficult circumstances, allowing *shalom* to grow within us and spread to others. Generosity is a willingness to share with others, to compassionately give to others. Christians are invited to "trust steadily in God, hope unswervingly [in God], love extravagantly" (1 Corinthians 13:13, *The Message*).

Enjoying beauty and a sense of awe and wonder

Taking time to choose to notice and appreciate the beauty around us cultivates feelings of awe, wonder and joy and has been shown to foster wellbeing.[80] This can be noticing and appreciating the beauty in nature, beauty in the compassion of others, beauty in creativity and art. For Christians, this can include a noticing and appreciation of who Jesus is and the blessings he offers. When Jesus was asked how we should pray, he gave the example: "Our Father in heaven . . . you're ablaze in beauty! Yes. Yes. Yes" (Matthew 6:7-13, *The Message*). This reveals the gift of joy through noticing and appreciating who God is.

The Book of Joy records the conversations between His Holiness the Dalai Lama and Archbishop Desmond Tutu as they reflected on the wisdom that they have gained from seeking to live their lives well through their respective religious faiths.[81] Both experienced profound personal suffering as well as the suffering of their communities. Both chose to dedicate their lives to be bearers of peace, compassion, justice and reconciliation to others' suffering. At the end of the book they conclude that authentic spirituality is revealed in how we relate to others. A life filled with joy stems from compassionate, meaningful and generous relationships with others. This life of joy touches and holds the potential to cultivate joy in others.

Dani, Jo and spiritual wellbeing

Dani's story in this chapter, along with Sam's and Jo's stories in the earlier chapters, illustrate many of the aspects related to spiritual wellbeing that are incorporated into the Wellbeing Zone table. Since we last visited Dani's story, some significant developments have occurred. The UK police have been able to work towards bringing her traffickers to justice, with the help of evidence from Dani and others. Although this process will take further time, Dani and the other survivors hope that their courage to give evidence will mean others will not have to experience the horrors they lived through. Also, the situation in Dani's home country has improved significantly, and Dani is now able to contemplate moving back and resuming her former life.

Dani has come to find the Wellbeing Zone's table and PEACE model help her to regularly pause and notice things about herself, such as the state of her physical health, the type of thoughts and feelings she is having and how she is relating to others. She has found the Wellbeing Zone resources help her to regulate herself and be proactive in cultivating her wellbeing. We've already seen how Dani has been able to grow in her ability to ask questions about herself, which has helped her develop a better sense of who she is after all the traumatic experiences and difficulties that she has lived through. She has survived the unimaginable and now has a deeper appreciation of the gift of each day and her life ahead.

When Jo met with Dani recently, aware that Dani was contemplating moving back to her home country, Jo suggested working through the PEACE model together with a focus on the Wellbeing Zone's spiritual life segment. Dani shared with Jo that the idea of returning home brought up many emotions and thoughts for her. She had changed, and in conversations with her family, she knew that they and her community had also changed, so she was unsure what "resuming" life there might be. Jo gently asked Dani to tell her more about what growing up in her family and community had been like, especially in terms of what beliefs and values were shared. Dani was able to explore with Jo the fusion of Buddhism and indigenous spiritual beliefs and practices that her family and community held, and how she especially absorbed the rule about compliance with the wishes of older family members so as not to bring shame upon the family. Exploring further, Dani realised that Buddhism had contributed to her love for the natural world, and noticed that from a young age she had been drawn to care for living things. More than that, she felt that she had a deep connection to nature, noticing the changes of the different seasons.

The experience of war and being trafficked, however, exposed Dani to a form of suffering and inhumane ways of treating people, which were contrary to the peaceful, accepting and compliant nature of her community back home during her childhood. The care shown to her by the charity and by Jo had gone some way to restore her faith in people, but she did not feel able, after all that had gone on, to simply return and fulfil the expectations of her elders. She told Jo she felt strongly that she did not want fear and shame to hold her back, and she had felt empowered by the courage it took for her to give evidence against her traffickers.

Jo reflected that when she first met Dani, Dani had seemed frightened and wanted to keep to herself, whereas now Jo had noticed the warmth and depth of sharing Dani had with a few of the other women who also attended regularly. Jo also shared that she had seen Dani's compassion towards several new women who had joined the wellbeing and garden groups. Dani recognised these changes in herself over the past two years and felt that the wellbeing group at the centre has helped her foster supportive relationships with other women who had had similar life experiences to herself. Dani also recognised that the care and support of the charity had helped her re-connect with herself as well as others. Dani felt she had grown into a woman who understood the balance between being able to make her own decisions and knowing when it is helpful to draw on the support of others to strengthen her wellbeing.

Dani shared with Jo that she was beginning to discover a new purpose and had realised that she wanted to work with young children as a teaching assistant, as she wanted to inspire and care for others. Dani had seen first-hand through Jo the impact of someone believing in you – how the peaceful, patient, kind presence of someone who genuinely cares for others could inspire others to hope too. Dani had wrestled with why she had lived through so much suffering over the past two years. It seemed so unfair and beyond her comprehension that in the world there was so much pain and destruction from war and people hurting others. She was grateful for the kindness and the altruism she'd seen in others, which gave rise to her sense of hope for her future.

As Jo reflected on her work with Dani with her manager Sam at the end of the day, Jo noticed that she felt a deep sense of gratitude to God and the Christian charity for the privilege of being in a role that brings her so much meaning and purpose in life. She recalled that when she first moved to London to begin university, she felt very alone and wondered where her desire to study psychology would lead her professionally. Although her personal life story was radically different from Dani's, Jo was aware her experience of feeling alone in a new country, alongside her childhood growing up in Dani's home country and speaking Dani's language, enabled a deep depth of compassionate empathy and relational connection with Dani. As Sam listened to Jo sharing her reflections, he reflected back that Jo, who was known for her peaceful, kind, joy-filled character, had grown considerably in her ability to support women who had experienced the trauma of being trafficked. Sam invited Jo to reflect on the growth she'd noticed within herself since beginning her role and Jo shared that she had developed a deeper appreciation of who she is as a person and how she can make a positive difference to others through compassionate care. Jo recognised that her peaceful, kind, joyful nature was the fruit of her Christian trust in God's compassion for her and her desire to follow the path that Jesus' life demonstrated, bringing compassion and peace to relationships.

Chapter 12

Continuing to nurture wellbeing and flourishing

As we noticed at the beginning, the Wellbeing Zone table includes a lot of information! We have looked at why each feature is included in the Wellbeing Zone table and how each one may contribute towards nurturing wellbeing. The topics we have touched on are hugely varied, as we've considered the central Christian theology as well as counselling and psychological theories that are woven into the Wellbeing Zone. If you are curious to discover more about a topic, the references offer a starting place for further reading. In selecting the references, I have tried to keep to keynote research and writing. I hope you will find the articles and books offer enjoyable and informative further discovery.

The Wellbeing Zone resources are designed to cultivate compassionate holistic understanding of the interrelated nature of our constantly changing wellbeing and survival responses as we adapt to external and our internal influences. You will have seen how the Wellbeing Zone provides a twin-targeted approach, enabling the consideration of how difficulties and distress may be best addressed alongside the consideration of how wellbeing and flourishing may be nurtured. By seeking to normalise survival reactions to stress or trauma, the Wellbeing Zone seeks to provide a base for non-judgemental compassionate responses. Compassionate understanding is the bedrock for all counselling and pastoral care initiatives. May I encourage you to continue asking the questions: "What has happened to me?" and "What has happened within me?" of yourself, and as you engage with and seek to care for others, to ask: "What has happened to you?" and "What is happening within you?" as you seek to integrate the Wellbeing Zone into your everyday professional, pastoral and personal lives. These questions contribute towards a trauma-informed care approach.

In this final chapter, I would like to reiterate two important points. Firstly, be mindful that trauma-informed approaches may inadvertently push a "helper" into an "expert" role. When using the Wellbeing Zone, it is important that a "helper" maintains the relational qualities described in the relational wellbeing zone, as these qualities reflect the qualities of trauma-informed care. The Wellbeing Zone resources are not to be imposed or prescribed. Rather, they are tools to be explored gently and by invitation. Secondly, as I stated in the introduction, the Wellbeing Zone is not a "cure" model. In the search to live well, particularly following distressing traumatic or abusive experiences, the help of specialist practitioners (including medical, counselling, other professionals and groups) may be required to achieve the sense of wellbeing much yearned for.

Utilising the Wellbeing Zone in daily life

If you haven't already done so, may I encourage you to have a go at using the Wellbeing Zone table and the Wellbeing Zone's PEACE and PRAY models and be compassionately curious as you do so. Choose a current situation in your life (either personal, pastoral or professional) in which you would like to better understand how to nurture your wellbeing. The PEACE and PRAY models both contain the same practical method to apply the skills of compassionate noticing, reflection, curiosity and creativity, so use whichever one you sense would work best for you. You might like to try them both. For those of you who want to use the resources with others, it is important that you use them first with yourself so you gain familiarity with the process of using them.

The Wellbeing Zone resources are designed to be used and have been used in a variety of contexts where trauma-informed care is required. We've seen with Sam, Jo and Dani how the Wellbeing Zone resources have been helpful in therapeutic supervision, developing organisational and team wellbeing, and for working either one-to-one or with groups to support the development of wellbeing and flourishing. The resources may be included in professional counselling. The PEACE and PRAY models are also designed so that they can be woven into Christian contemplative practices, which have played an integral part of Christian spiritual formation and seeking to grow in living life following Jesus' example. The practices aim to provide a structure to be present in the presence of God in loving awareness.

Professional counsellors and therapeutic supervisors will no doubt recognise and be familiar with many or all of the theories and skills embedded in the Wellbeing Zone. Please feel welcome to adapt the resources to the unique needs of the people and contexts that you are working or serving with. I have highlighted the necessity of sensitivity to a person's individual language when using the Wellbeing Zone table and resources. Individual experiences must not be fitted into the language used in the table; instead, respect must be given to a person's unique telling of their story. I have also highlighted that a person's culture will shape how they may respond to an event, necessitating the need to adapt and expand the Wellbeing Zone's descriptions to fit the cultural context.

The British Chief Rabbi Lord Jonathan Sacks in his book *The Great Partnership: God, Science and the Search for Meaning* asserts that the greatest belief to have inspired humanity is the belief that the world was created in love by the God who also invites humanity to create in love.[82] We've discussed in chapter two how Jesus responded to the beheading of John the Baptist in ways that fostered the wellbeing and flourishing of others, both those close to Jesus, his disciples, and those further away – the crowd following him. My hope is that the Wellbeing Zone and the related resources will help in fostering compassionate responses when attending to the impact of psychological trauma and the nurturing of wellbeing and flourishing for all, that they may contribute to "showing us the way, one foot at a time, down the path of peace" (Luke 1:79, *The Message*).

If you would like to discover more about how Jesus' life seeks to bring *shalom*, may I invite you to consider reading or listening to the Gospels? The four Gospels take about ten hours to read or about eight hours to listen to. Mark's Gospel is the shortest account of Jesus' life. As you read or listen to the Gospels, what do you notice about Jesus offering a pathway to peace and wellbeing in life? May I invite you to reflect on what you notice, to be curious, to perhaps use the PEACE or PRAY models as you read or listen?

As this book comes to an end, I invite us to draw on the words of Jesus: "Shalom I leave with you; my shalom I give you" (John 14:27, Tree of Life Version) as we seek to grow in nurturing wellbeing, flourishing and *shalom* in our relationships with ourselves, with others and with nature.

I wish you *shalom*.

Sarah

Appendices

Appendix A

The Wellbeing Zone table

WELLBEING ZONE TABLE

	HYPER-AROUSAL ZONE Fight-or-flight response	WELLBEING ZONE Befriending response	HYPO-AROUSAL ZONE Freeze-or-fold response
Physical life	Increase in adrenaline; raised heart and breathing rate, blood redirected to muscles, shaking; surge in energy then exhaustion; activation of neurobiological survival responses; increasing vulnerability to stress-related health conditions and diseases; difficulties in sleeping.	Proactive to physical health needs; sense of strength, alertness and energy as health allows.	Exhaustion; lethargy; fatigue; burnout; rundown; neglecting or struggling to be proactive in attending to physical health needs; vulnerable to sickness.
Emotional life	Increasing anxiety, stress, panic, frustration or mis-projected anger. Feeling restless, on-edge, overwhelmed or unsafe; over-reactive; emotional flooding.	Awareness, acceptance and understanding of feelings; being able to respond to emotions that enables wellbeing of self and others; feelings correspond to the situation; compassion; gratitude; hope; empathic to self and others; sense of inner peace.	Feeling low, flat, self-absorbed, depressed, or numb; feelings of shame, disconnection, isolation, helplessness, losing hope; feeling depleted and struggling to be compassionate to self and others; struggling to sense reality and a vulnerability to disconnect from reality.
Thinking life	Becoming focused on past and/or future events; losing perspective; self-absorbed; struggling to think clearly, remember, make decisions or mind going blank or going around in circles; becoming obsessive, judgemental and rigid; catastrophising; narrative may be inconsistent, confusing or incomplete. Distressing memories, intrusive images.	Able to think clearly, objectively and realistically; consider others' perspective and own; thinking is open to new ideas and information; problem solving; able to be reflective; curious and creative; able to give an understandable consistent narrative.	Dwelling on the past and/or future; becoming pulled towards a negative focus, fixed positions, self-absorbed; cynicism; struggling to think clearly, make decisions or going blank; going around in circles; narrative may be inconsistent, confusing, incomplete; vulnerability to dissociate from reality.

Behavioural life	Becoming increasingly obsessive, repetitive, impulsive, hostile, on edge or hyper-vigilant; vulnerable to numbing, spacing-out or addictions.	Attuned to the present moment; responses adapting to the situation to enable the wellbeing and flourishing of self, others and creation; consideration of the past, present and future; courageous; taking initiative; being able to delay gratification; ability to play; creativity.	Becoming passive, withdrawn, isolating and shutdown; drawn towards numbing, spacing out or addictions; operating on autopilot.
Relational life	Becoming increasingly over-reactive, agitated, defensive, avoiding, dominating, demanding, critical, intolerant, exploitative, abusive, self-absorbed or anxious towards others; inclination towards compulsive caretaking or controlling of others; disregarding relational boundaries.	Attunement to and proactive in the development of relationships where all can flourish; sense of relational peace; awareness of and maintenance of healthy relational boundaries; being able to form inter-dependent relationships that are collaborative, accountable and respectful with intimacy and commitment; being humble, tolerant, honest and genuine.	Becoming avoidant, detached, ambivalent, rejecting or dependent in relationships; self-absorbed; vulnerable to others' control, neglect or abuse; losing ability to defend self, initiate responsibility and care of self and others; vulnerability to be unable to maintain healthy boundaries; tendency to be critical of others; struggle to receive affirmation; vulnerability to dissociate from reality.
Spiritual life	Losing the capacity to form and connect with core beliefs, values and sustaining practices that recognise self and others hold infinite worth and care for nature; losing sense of peace, joy and mystery; becoming entitled, impatient and exploitative; struggling to give and receive forgiveness; losing ability to enjoy beauty and sense of awe and wonder; at risk of radicalisation.	Having the capacity to form and connect with core beliefs, values and sustaining practices during suffering and everyday life that recognise self and others hold infinite worth and care of nature; nurturing peace and wellbeing for self and all; giving and receiving forgiveness; accepting mystery; seeking justice for all; holding qualities of hope, compassion, patience, gratitude, generosity and kindness; enjoying beauty and sense of awe and wonder. Altruism.	Losing the capacity to form and connect with core beliefs, values and sustaining practices that recognise self and others hold infinite worth and care for nature; increasing compassion fatigue in care of self, others and creation; becoming bitter; vulnerable to injustice and moral injury; struggling to give and receive forgiveness; sensing emptiness, hopelessness, despair and life is meaningless; struggling to notice and enjoy beauty; losing of sense of awe and wonder.

KEY: Each of us will have a range of unique experiences. We may not experience everything described. This chart is a visual presentation to assist in compassionate awareness and understanding, alongside comprehensive and ongoing assessment. It is not to be used diagnostically or prescriptively. Copyright © Sarah Armitage

WELLBEING ZONE TABLE

	HYPER-AROUSAL ZONE Fight-or-flight response	WELLBEING ZONE Befriending response	HYPO-AROUSAL ZONE Fold-or-freeze response
Physical life	Increase in adrenaline; raised heart and breathing rate, blood redirected to muscles, shaking; surge in energy then exhaustion; activation of neurobiological survival responses; increasing vulnerability to stress-related health conditions and diseases; difficulties in sleeping.	Proactive to physical health needs; sense of strength, alertness and energy as health allows.	Exhaustion; lethargy; fatigue; burnout; rundown; neglecting or struggling to be proactive in attending to physical health needs; vulnerable to sickness.
Emotional life	Increasing anxiety, stress, panic, frustration or mis-projected anger. Feeling restless, on-edge, overwhelmed or unsafe; over-reactive; emotional flooding.	Awareness, acceptance and understanding of feelings; being able to respond to emotions that enables wellbeing of self and others; feelings correspond to the situation; compassion; gratitude; hope; empathic to self and others; sense of inner peace.	Feeling low, flat, self-absorbed, depressed, or numb; feelings of shame, disconnection, isolation, helplessness, losing hope; feeling depleted and struggling to be compassionate to self and others; struggling to sense reality and a vulnerability to disconnect from reality.
Thinking life	Becoming focused on past and/or future events; losing perspective; self-absorbed; struggling to think clearly, remember, make decisions or mind going blank or going around in circles; becoming obsessive, judgemental and rigid; catastrophising; narrative may be inconsistent, confusing or incomplete. Distressing memories, intrusive images.	Able to think clearly, objectively and realistically; consider others' perspective and own; thinking is open to new ideas and information; problem solving; able to be reflective; curious and creative; able to give an understandable consistent narrative.	Dwelling on the past and/or future; becoming pulled towards a negative focus, fixed positions, self-absorbed; cynicism; struggling to think clearly, make decisions or going blank; going around in circles; narrative may be inconsistent, confusing, incomplete; vulnerability to dissociate from reality.

Behavioural life	Becoming increasingly obsessive, repetitive, impulsive, hostile, on edge or hyper-vigilant; vulnerable to numbing, spacing-out or addictions.	Attuned to the present moment; responses adapting to the situation to enable the wellbeing and flourishing of self, others and creation; consideration of the past, present and future; courageous; taking initiative; being able to delay gratification; ability to play; creativity.	Becoming passive, withdrawn, isolating and shutdown; drawn towards numbing, spacing out or addictions; operating on autopilot.
Relational life	Becoming increasingly over-reactive, agitated, defensive, avoiding, dominating, demanding, critical, intolerant, exploitative, abusive, self-absorbed or anxious towards others; inclination towards compulsive caretaking or controlling of others; disregarding relational boundaries.	Attunement to and proactive in the development of relationships where all can flourish; sense of relational peace; awareness of and maintenance of healthy relational boundaries; being able to form inter-dependent relationships that are collaborative, accountable and respectful with intimacy and commitment; being humble, tolerant, honest and genuine.	Becoming avoidant, detached, ambivalent, rejecting or dependent in relationships; self-absorbed; vulnerable to others' control, neglect or abuse; losing ability to defend self, initiate responsibility and care of self and others; vulnerability to be unable to maintain healthy boundaries; tendency to be critical of others; struggle to receive affirmation; vulnerability to dissociate from reality.
Spiritual life	Losing the capacity to form and connect with core beliefs, values and sustaining practices that recognise self and others hold infinite worth and care for nature; losing sense of peace, joy and mystery; becoming entitled, impatient and exploitative; struggling to give and receive forgiveness; losing ability to enjoy beauty and sense of awe and wonder; at risk of radicalisation.	Having the capacity to form and connect with core beliefs, values and sustaining practices during suffering and everyday life that recognise self and others hold infinite worth and care of nature; nurturing peace and wellbeing for self and all; giving and receiving forgiveness; accepting mystery; seeking justice for all; holding qualities of hope, compassion, patience, gratitude, generosity and kindness; enjoying beauty and sense of awe and wonder. Altruism.	Losing the capacity to form and connect with core beliefs, values and sustaining practices that recognise self and others hold infinite worth and care for nature; increasing compassion fatigue in care of self, others and creation; becoming bitter; vulnerable to injustice and moral injury; struggling to give and receive forgiveness; sensing emptiness, hopelessness, despair and life is meaningless; struggling to notice and enjoy beauty; losing of sense of awe and wonder.

KEY: Each of us will have a range of unique experiences. We may not experience everything described. This chart is a visual presentation to assist in compassionate awareness and understanding, alongside comprehensive and ongoing assessment. It is not to be used diagnostically or prescriptively. Copyright © Sarah Armitage

Appendix B

The Wellbeing Zone PEACE Model

When using the PEACE model, you might find it helpful to have a copy of the Wellbeing Zone table and template, the PEACE model template, Wellbeing Zone personal and/or team plan and a journal at hand to note down your initial observations, reflections and questions. This can be helpful to refer to as well as notice any changes as you seek to develop your wellbeing. At first, the skill of noticing can be difficult. Like learning any new skill, the more we practise, the more we become able to improve and use the skills in everyday life. You may find it helpful to find somewhere quiet, or you may find it helpful to go through the PEACE model with someone. Take time to *reflect* on what you've *noticed* and then move on to the *curiosity* and *creativity* steps, which are in the "Ask" and "Create" steps of the PEACE model. The Wellbeing Zone personal plan can be used to record possible ways that you can nurture your wellbeing and flourishing across the different areas of your life. There is also a Wellbeing

Zone team plan for when the Wellbeing Zone is being used with teams. It is helpful to regularly review, perhaps weekly at first, the impact of any changes that you have made to help nurture your wellbeing, and then adapt your plan accordingly.

Appendix B

Pause	Take a few steady breaths, breathing in through your nose for the count of four, holding your breath for the count of four, then breathing out through your nose for the count of four, resting for the count of four and then repeating the cycle several times. Now take time to notice your physical body. How do the different parts of your body feel? You may like to begin at your toes and move up through your body to your head, noticing any signs of tension, discomfort or ease. Reflect on your energy levels, overall health, daily sleep, rest, diet and exercise patterns. Then move your noticing to your emotional, thinking, behavioural, relational and spiritual life. Ask yourself these questions: What feelings do I notice? We often can feel a mixture of feelings at the same time. What do I notice about the thoughts I am having now? Are these thoughts generally hopeful and do they nurture wellbeing and flourishing, or are they distressing? Is there a pattern to my thoughts and if so, what might this pattern be? What patterns of behaviour am I drawn towards? What do I notice about how I am relating to others? What do I notice about my spiritual life? What do I notice about how my feelings, thoughts, behaviours, ways of relating and my spiritual life impact on one another?
Enquire	How would I describe what I notice? How does this relate to the descriptions in the Wellbeing Zone? Which zones (hyper-arousal, hypo-arousal or wellbeing) do I sense I am in for each of the areas of my life?
Ask	What do I and others desire or need to help nurture wellbeing and flourishing?
Create	What resources can I draw on? What new skills or changes would be helpful to develop? How could I do this? When could I start to do this?
Engage	What compassionate choice(s) can I make to nurture wellbeing and flourishing? How do my choices nurture others and their wellbeing and flourishing? How do my choices care for nature?

Wellbeing Zone PEACE model template

Pause	
Enquire	
Ask	
Create	
Engage	

Appendix C

The Wellbeing Zone PRAY model

When using the PRAY model, you might find it helpful to have a copy of the Wellbeing Zone table and template, the PRAY model template, Wellbeing Zone personal and/or team plan and a journal at hand to note down your initial observations, reflections and questions. This can be helpful to refer to as well as notice any changes as you seek to develop your wellbeing. At first, the skill of noticing can be difficult. Like learning any new skill, the more we practise, the more we become able to improve and use the skills in everyday life. You may find it helpful to find somewhere quiet, or you may find it helpful to go through the PRAY model with someone. Take time to *reflect* on what you've *noticed* and then move on to the *curiosity* and *creativity* steps, which are in the "Ask" and "Create" steps of the PRAY model. The Wellbeing Zone personal plan can be used to record possible ways that you can nurture your wellbeing and flourishing across the different areas of your life. There is also a Wellbeing Zone team plan for when the Wellbeing Zone is being used with teams. It is helpful to regularly review, perhaps weekly at first, the impact of any changes that you have made to help nurture your wellbeing, and then adapt your plan accordingly.

Pause	Take a few steady breaths, breathing in through your nose for the count of four, holding this breath for the count of four, then breathing out through your nose for the count of four, resting for the count of four and then repeating the cycle several times. Now take time to notice your physical body. How do the different parts of your body feel? You may like to begin at your toes and move up through your body to your head, noticing any signs of tension, discomfort or ease. Reflect on your energy levels, overall health, daily sleep, rest, diet and exercise patterns.
	Then move your noticing to your emotional, thinking, behavioural, relational, and spiritual life. Ask yourself these questions:
	What feelings do I notice? We often can feel a mixture of feelings at the same time.
	What do I notice about the thoughts I am having now? Are these thoughts generally hopeful and do they nurture wellbeing and flourishing, or are they distressing? Is there a pattern to my thoughts and if so, what might this pattern be?
	What patterns of behaviour am I drawn towards?
	What do I notice about how I am relating to others?
	What do I notice about my spiritual life?
	What do I notice about how my feelings, thoughts, behaviours, ways of relating and my spiritual life impact on one another?
Reflect	How would I describe what I notice?
	How does this relate to the descriptions in the Wellbeing Zone?
	Which zones (hyper-arousal, hypo-arousal or wellbeing) do I sense I am in for each of the areas of my life?
Ask	What do I and others desire or need to help nurture wellbeing and flourishing?
	What resources can I draw on?
	What new skills or changes would be helpful to develop?
	How could I do this?
	When could I start to do this?
Yield	What compassionate choice(s) can I make to nurture wellbeing and flourishing?
	How do my choices nurture others and their wellbeing and flourishing?
	How do my choices care for nature?

Wellbeing Zone PRAY model template

Pause	
Reflect	
Ask	
Yield	

Appendix D

The Wellbeing Zone personal plan can be used to record possible ways that you can nurture your wellbeing and flourishing across the different areas of your life. There is also a Wellbeing Zone team plan for when the Wellbeing Zone is being used with teams. As you consider how to nurture your wellbeing and flourishing, include resources that are already available and any new resources that would be helpful. Try to make your plan realistic to your circumstances.

It is helpful to regularly review, perhaps weekly at first, the impact of any changes that you made to help nurture your wellbeing, and then adapt your plan accordingly.

The Wellbeing Zone personal plan

Life area	Ways I will continue to nurture wellbeing and flourishing
Physical life	
Emotional life	
Thinking life	
Behavioural life	
Relational life	
Spiritual life	

The Wellbeing Zone team plan

Life area	How we will nurture wellbeing and flourishing
Physical life	
Emotional life	
Thinking life	
Behavioural life	
Relational life	
Spiritual life	

Appendix E

The Wellbeing Zone wheel of emotions

The Wellbeing Zone's wheel of emotions assists in noticing and naming the emotions present in our emotional life. Understanding our emotional life brings much insight into how we are experiencing life and provides a starting point to then consider how we may nurture our wellbeing.

The colours reflect the colours in the Wellbeing Zone table: red are emotions that can arise when we are in the hyper-arousal zone; blue are the emotions that can arise when we are in the hypo-arousal zone; green and yellow are emotions that correlate with the wellbeing zone.

We can often be feeling several emotions at the same time. As you look at the emotions named in the wheel, which ones do you sense you are experiencing either now or at a time in the past? If the emotions named on the wheel don't accurately reflect what you are or were feeling, consider what word or words do reflect your emotional life. It can take a while to become aware of and accurately name the emotions we are feeling, particularly in distressing, confusing or overwhelming situations.

The eight segments on the wheel are matched with opposite emotions. For example, the opposite of anxiety is peace. Once you've noticed and named the emotions that you are feeling, you may like to use the Wellbeing Zone's PEACE or PRAY models to guide your understanding as to what may be the root cause of the emotion and what would be helpful for you to nurture your wellbeing and flourishing. When you are experiencing emotions in the red hyper-arousal or blue hypo-arousal segments, as part of your consideration of what fosters your wellbeing, you may find it helpful to choose a corresponding opposite emotion in the green or yellow wellbeing zone segments and consider how you may nurture that emotion.

Appendix E

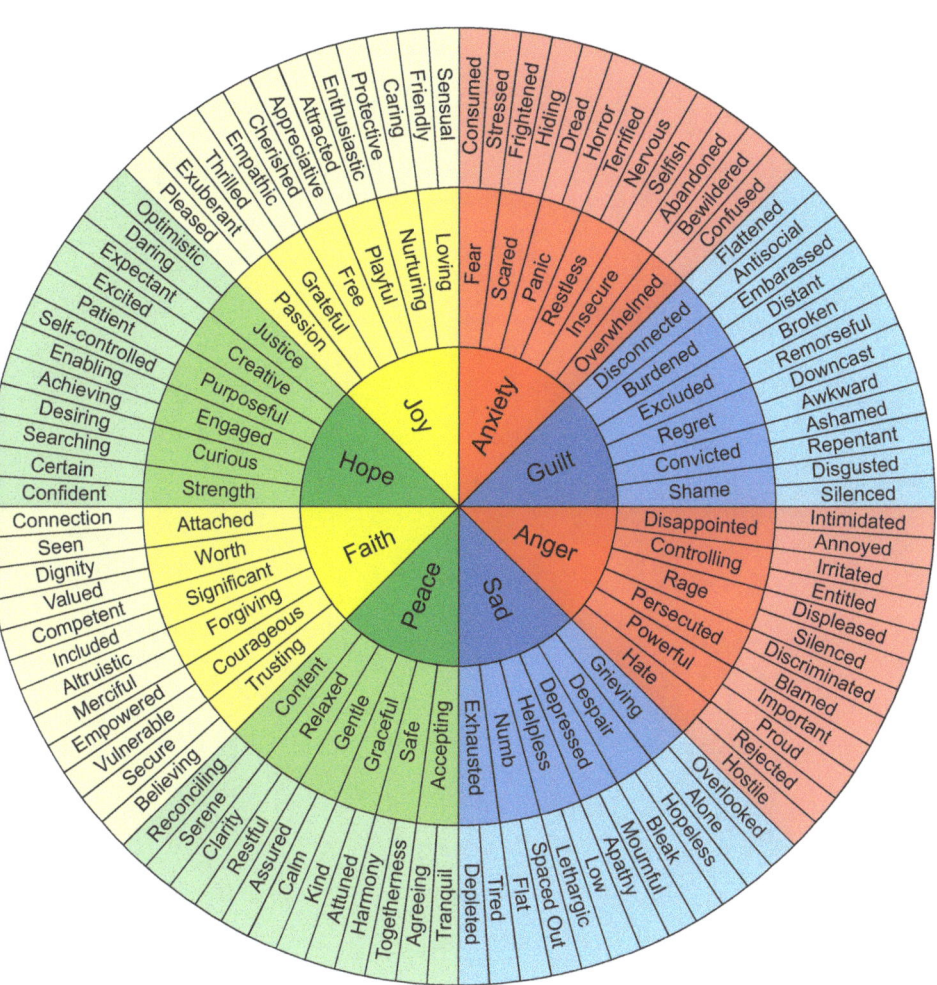

Appendix F

The Wellbeing Zone table of common thinking distortions

THINKING DISTORTION	DESCRIPTION OF THE THINKING DISTORTION	RESPONDING TO THE THINKING DISTORTION
Catastrophising	Worst-case scenario thinking, scanning for every possible potential worst outcome.	Consider: what is the evidence for these potential scenarios? What is realistically most likely to happen?
Emotional reasoning	I feel it so it must be true.	Bear in mind our feelings are due to how we interpret an event, so ask: Are my interpretations accurate? Can I consider different interpretations?
Expert	Assuming what works in one situation will also work in all other situations.	Remember each situation/topic is unique; consider other people's input.
Globalising	Labelling everything or people as the same, often negatively.	Respect that everyone is unique; things are complex and made up of many parts.
Low tolerance	Magnifying the difficulties or emotional pain and minimising your coping skills.	Consider potential resources and support to enable a stepped approach to challenges.
Microscopic	Focusing on one small part, which then rules the overall outlook.	Consider the bigger picture, the wider context.
Mind-reading	Assuming others are thinking negatively about you.	Remember no one fully knows another's thoughts. Consider asking for or inviting feedback.
Minimising	To make negative impact seem smaller or less important.	Consider the full impact and consequences of the situation/event.
Negative focus	Focus on the negative and overlook the positive or what is OK in the situation.	Consider what may be the positives or the OK in the situation.
Othering	Labelling people into groups having different characteristics from you.	Honouring the unique value of each person. Being welcoming to others who may be different from you.
Personalising	Taking total responsibility or blame for distressing events.	Consider explanations that do not involve you, the bigger picture, other contributing factors or how others have contributed.
Polarised thinking	Thinking in polar opposites, something is either all good or all bad.	Recognise life is complex, rarely is something all good or all bad. Remember good can come out of bad situations, and good things can have negative parts.
Quickest route	Focusing only on the quickest route, to get something done as quickly as possible.	Consider and evaluate other ways of responding.

Template to nurture wellbeing in our thinking life

Our brains are constantly seeking to understand internal and external events. Each day we have around 70,000–100,000 automatic thoughts. That's a lot of automatic thoughts! When our thinking life is in the hypo- or hyper-arousal zone, our automatic thoughts will often have a negative and unhelpful focus. This can lead to a pattern of thoughts forming. Such patterns are called "thinking distortions". These thinking distortions lead to distress in our thinking and in our other areas of life.

The skill of being able to compassionately observe our thinking life and identify a thinking distortion provides a base from which to either challenge, modify or refrain from responding to unhelpful thoughts and, in doing so, nurture our wellbeing. Learning to challenge our negative automatic thoughts with a thought that helps foster wellbeing enables our thought life to nurture our wellbeing.

In the table on page 235, the left-hand column describes different types of thinking distortions. The middle column offers a description of the thinking distortion. As you read down the left-hand and middle columns, notice which type of thinking distortions you experience more often, particularly when you are tired or feeling low or stressed. The right-hand column offers a way of challenging the thinking distortion. When you next notice your thoughts are following a thinking distortion, challenge the thinking distortion with the corresponding question or thought in the right-hand column. You may find it helpful to write out the frequent thinking distortions that come into your thought life and then write out how you will challenge them so that you are prepared for when you next notice a thinking distortion.

Appendix F

Thought, thinking distortions and related emotions	Compassionate alternatives to the thinking distortion and related emotion	What can I do to be compassionate to myself and others?
For example: **Thought:** "No one will speak to me at the party as they think I'm boring." **Thinking distortions:** Catastrophising Globalising Mind-reading Negative focus **Related emotions:** Anxiety	"I have been friends with Tom (the party host) for a year and we share fun conversations." "It is normal at a party that some people will be more extrovert and chatty and some more shy, like me. Just because I take a while to feel at ease with new people doesn't mean I am boring." "I have no evidence that the other guests will think I'm boring as they haven't met me yet." "Everyone knows the party host in some way so I could begin a conversation with 'How do you know Tom?' and ask about their life." **Related emotions:** I am feeling a little nervous, however also looking forward to seeing Tom and curious to meet his other friends.	I will remind myself of the compassionate alternative thoughts on the journey to the party and during the party. If I feel anxious on the journey I will do my relaxation breathing. I will remind myself that we are all different and that it is OK to be shyer than others. If I see another guest on their own, I will introduce myself and ask, "How do you know Tom?" I can ask Tom if there is anything I can do to help with the party.

Appendix G

Wellbeing Zone table template

Have a copy of the Wellbeing Zone table to refer to, to help you identify which column (red hyper-arousal, green wellbeing or blue hypo-arousal) your observations are in and then record your observations in the different areas of your life on this Wellbeing Zone template. You are welcome to use your own descriptions. Once you've done this, use the PEACE or PRAY model to help you consider how you may nurture your wellbeing.

WELLBEING ZONE TABLE

	HYPER-AROUSAL ZONE Fight-or-flight response	WELLBEING ZONE Befriending response	HYPO-AROUSAL ZONE Freeze-or-fold response
PHYSICAL LIFE			
EMOTIONAL LIFE			
THINKING LIFE			

BEHAVIOURAL LIFE			
RELATIONAL LIFE			
SPIRITUAL LIFE			

KEY: Each of us will have a range of unique experiences. We may not experience everything described. This chart is a visual presentation to assist in compassionate awareness and understanding, alongside comprehensive and ongoing assessment. It is not to be used diagnostically or prescriptively. Copyright © Sarah Armitage

Endnotes

1. Armitage, S. (2022) "The Wellbeing Zone", *accord.* Winter 2022/2023 (issue no. 117), pp 4-8.

2. Stewart-Brown, S., Platt, S., Tennant, A. & Maheswaran, H. (2011) "The Warwick-Edinburgh Mental Wellbeing Scale (WEMWBS): A valid and reliable tool for measuring mental well-being in diverse populations and projects", *Journal of Epidemiology and Community Health*, September Vol. 65, pp. A38-A39.

3. Greig, P. (2019) *How to Pray*. London: Hodder & Stoughton Ltd.

4. Siegal, D. (2018) *Aware*. London: Scribe Publications, pp. 23-27.

5. Siegal, D. (2018) *Aware*. London: Scribe Publications, pp. 46-47.

6. Goetz, J. & Simon-Thomas, E. (2017) "The Landscape of Compassion: Definitions and scientific approaches." Pages 3-16. In (ed) Seppala, E., Simon-Thomas, E., Brown, S., Worline, M., Cameron, C. & Doty, J. eds. *The Oxford Handbook of Compassion Science*. Oxford: Oxford University Press.

7. Gilbert, P., Catarino, F., Duarte, C., Matos, M., Kolts, R., Stubbs, J., Ceresatto, L., Duarte, J., Pinto-Gouveia, J. & Basran, J. (2017) "The Development of Compassionate Engagement and Action Scales for Self and Others", *Journal of Compassionate Health Care*, Vol. 4. Article No. 4, pp. 1-24.

8. Luft, J. & Ingham, H. (1955) "The Johari Window, a graphic model of interpersonal awareness", *Proceedings of the Western Training Laboratory in Group Development.* Los Angeles: University of California.

9. Jernigan, H. (2001) "Spirituality in Older Adults: A cross-cultural and interfaith perspective", *Pastoral Psychology*, Vol. 49, pp. 418.

10. Pope Francis, (2015) "Laudato si – on care for our common home". Vatican. paragraph 217.

11. Sheldrake, P. (2013) *Spirituality: A Brief History.* Chichester: John Wiley & Sons Ltd. Glossary, pp. 138.

12. Holtam, N. (2022) *Sleepers Wake: Getting Serious About Climate Change.* London: SPCK, pp. 6.

13. Fisher, J. (2011) "The Four Domains Model: Connecting spirituality, health and well-being", *Religions.* Dec. 2, pp. 22.

14. Wilson, J. & Lindy, J. (2013) *Trauma, Culture and Metaphor.* Hove: Routledge, pp. 97,113.

15. Frechette, C. & Boase, E. (2016) *Bible Through the Lens of Trauma.* Atlanta: SBL Press.

16. Evans, H. (2021) "Complex trauma and post-traumatic growth", *accord.* Summer 2021 (issue no. 11), pp. 4-10.

17. Cook, C. & Hamley, I. (2020) *The Bible and Mental Health.* London: SCM Press.

18. Glasson, B. (2009) *A Spirituality of Survival.* London: Continuum International Publishing Group.

19. Horsfall, T. & Hawker, D. (2019) *Resilience in Life and Faith.* Abingdon: The Bible Reading Fellowship.

20. American Psychiatric Association (1980) *The Diagnostic and Statistical Manual of Mental Disorders (DSM).* 3rd edition. Arlington: American Psychiatric Association.

21. Office for Health Improvement & Disparities. (2022) *Guidance: Working Definition of Trauma-informed Practice.* Available at: www.gov.uk/government/publications/working-definition-of-trauma-informed-practice/working-definition-of-trauma-informed-practice (Accessed: 17/01/25).

22. Siegal, D. (2020) *The Developing Mind.* London: The Guildford Press.

23. Fisher, J. (2017) *Healing the Fragmented Selves of Trauma Survivors.* New York: Routledge, pp. 77-102.

24. Lahad, M., Shacham, M. & Ayalon, O. (2013) *The "BASIC Ph" Model of Coping and Resiliency.* London: Jessica Kingsley Publishing, pp. 22-25.

25. Frankl, V. (2004) *Man's Search for Meaning*. London: Hodder & Stoughton Ltd, pp. 74,77.

26. Younie, L. (2020) "When I say Flourishing in Medical Education", *Journal of Holistic Healthcare*, 17(3),pp. 44-46.

27. Seligman, M. (2011) *Flourish*. London: Nicholas Brealey Publications. pp. 24.

28. Freudenberger, H. J. (1975). "The Staff Burn-out Syndrome in Alternative Institutions", *Psychotherapy: Theory, Research & Practice, 12*(1), pp. 73-82.

29. Maslach, C. & Leiter, M. (2016) "Understanding the Burnout Experience: Recent Research and its Implications for Psychiatry", *World Psychiatry*, 15(2), pp. 103-111.

30. Maslach, C. & Jackson, S. (1981) "The measurement of experienced burnout", *Journal of Occupational Behaviour*, Vol. 2, pp. 99-113.

31. Lomaz, T. (2021) "Life balance and harmony: Wellbeing's golden thread", *International Journal of Wellbeing*, April 2021, pp. 18-36.

32. Tedeschi, R. & Calhorn, L. (1996) "The posttraumatic growth inventory: Measuring the positive legacy of trauma", *Journal of Traumatic Stress*, 9(3), pp. 455-471.

33. Tedeschi, R. (2020) "Growth after trauma", *Harvard Business Review*, July–August 2021. Available at: hbr.org/2020/07/growth-after-trauma (Accessed: 1/11/24).

34. Hobfoll, S.E., Watson, P., Bell, C.C., Bryant R.A., Brymer, M.J., Friedman, M.J., et al. (2007) "Five essential elements of immediate and mid-term mass trauma intervention: Empirical evidence", *Psychiatry*, No. 70, pp. 283-315.

35. Zohar, J., Sonnino, R., Juven-Wetzler, A., Cwikel-Hamzany, S., Balaban, E., Cohen, H. (2011) "New insights into secondary prevention in post-traumatic stress disorder", *Dialogues in Clinical Neuroscience*, No.13, pp. 301-309.

36. WHO (1946) *Constitution of the World Health Organisation*. Available at: www.who.int/about/governance/constitution (Accessed: 17/01/25).

37. Mate, G. (2019) *When the Body Says No*. London: Penguin Random House.

38. van der Kolk, B. (2015) *The Body Keeps the Score*. London: Penguin Random House.

39. Plutchik, R. (1980) *A General Psychoevolutionary Theory of Emotion*. New York: Academic Press, pp. 3-33.

40. Swinton, J, (2018) *Raging with Compassion*. London: SCM Press.

41. Keller, T. (2018) *My Rock My Refuge*. London: Hodder & Stoughton.

42. Brueggemann, W. (2007) *Praying the Psalms*. 2nd edition. Eugene: Cascade Books.

43. Wood, A., Froh, J. & Geraghty, A. (2010) "Gratitude and well-being: A review and theoretical integration", *Clinical Psychology Review*, 30(7), pp. 890-905.

44. Emmons, R. & Mishra, A. (2011) "Why gratitude enhances well-being: What we need to know" in Sheldon et al. (eds.). *Designing Positive Psychology*. Oxford: Oxford University Press, Chapter 16, pp. 248-262.

45. Stead, T. (2016) *Mindfulness and Christian Spirituality*. London: SPCK.

46. Stead, T. (2018) *See, Love, Be – Mindfulness and the Spiritual Life*. London: SPCK.

47. Beck, A. (1979) *Cognitive Therapy and the Emotional Disorders*. London: Penguin Publishing Group.

48. A. Ellis, (1991) "The Revised ABC's of Rational-emotive Therapy (RET)", *Journal of Rational-Emotive and Cognitive-Behavioural Therapy*, Vol. 9, pp. 139-172.

49. Reivich. K, & Shatte, A. (2002) *The Resilience Factor*. New York: Three Rivers Press.

50. Gerhardt, S. (2014) *Why Love Matters: How affection shapes a baby's brain*. Hove: Routledge.

51. Cozolino, L. (2006) *The Neuroscience of Human Relationships*. New York: W.W. Norton & Company, Inc.

52. Thompson, C. (2010) *Anatomy of the Soul*. Carol Stream: Tyndale House Publishers.

53. Lindsay, B. (2019) *We Need to Talk About Race*. London: SPCK, pp. 24-26,77.

54. Olthuis, J. (2001) *The Beautiful Risk.* Eugene: Wipf and Stock Publishers, pp. 48.

55. McLean, S. (2023) *McLean's ABC Cultural Competency Model: A Culturally Directed Workbook.* Business With Excellence.

56. Williams, R. (2018) *Being Human.* London: SPCK.

57. Fowler, J. (1981) *Stages of Faith.* New York: Harper Collins.

58. Liquin, E., Metz, S.E., Lombrozo, T. (2020) "Science demands explanation, religion tolerates mystery", *Science Direct*, Vol. 204. Available at: www.sciencedirect.com/science/article/pii/S0010027720302171 (Accessed: 21/8/24).

59. The origin of the Serenity Prayer. Available at: www.aahistory.com/prayer.html (Accessed 17/01/25). Reinhold Niebuhr is considered the author of the Serenity Prayer.

60. Keller, T. (2015) *Walking with God Through Pain & Suffering.* London: Hodder & Stoughton Ltd, pp. 174.

61. Plyming, P. (2023) *Being Real: The Apostle Paul's Hardship Narratives and the Stories We Tell Today.* London: SCM Press, pp. 70.

62. Thirtyoneeight – Publications: research reports, review reports, reference documents. Available at: thirtyoneeight.org/help-and-resources/publications/ (Accessed: 17/01/25).

63. Oakley, L. & Humphreys, J. (2019) *Escaping the Maze of Spiritual Abuse*. London: SPCK.

64. Kruger, M. (2022) *Bully Pulpit: Confronting the Problem of Spiritual Abuse in the Church*. Grand Rapids: Zondervan.

65. De Groat, C. (2020) *When Narcissism Comes to Church*. Downers Grove: Inter-Varsity Press.

66. Litz, B., Lebowitz, L., Gray, M. & Nash, W. (2018) *Adaptive Disclosure: A New Treatment for Military Trauma, Loss, and Moral Injury.* London: The Guildford Press.

67. Koenig, H. & Zaben, F. (2021) "Moral Injury: An increasingly recognized and widespread syndrome", *Journal of Religious Health*, 60(5), pp. 2,980-3,011.

68. Litz, B., Lebowitz, L., Gray, M. & Nash, W. (2018) *Adaptive Disclosure: A New Treatment for Military Trauma, Loss, and Moral Injury.* London: The Guildford Press, pp. 17,18.

69. Churchill, H. (2021) "The Churchill Framework", *accord*, Spring 2021 (issue no. 110), pp. 21-27.

70. Schut, M. (1999) "The dual process model of coping with bereavement: Rationale and description", *Death Studies*. 23(3), pp. 197-224.

71. Reivich. K, & Shatte, A. (2002) *The Resilience Factor*. New York: Three Rivers Press.

72. Lichtenfeld, S., Maier, M., Buechner, V. & Capo, M. (2019) "The influence of decisional and emotional forgiveness on attributions", *Frontiers in Psychology*, Vol. 10. Article 1425.

73. Tuto, D. & Tuto, M. (2015) *The Book of Forgiving*. London: William Collins.

74. Luskin, F. (2003) *Forgive for Good*. New York: Harper Collins.

75. Support and care for when you or someone else is feeling suicidal:

    NHS – Call 999 if emergency services are needed or go straight to A&E, or ask someone else to call 999 or take you to A&E.

    Call a GP – ask for an emergency appointment.

    Call 111 out of hours medical care.

    Contact your NHS mental health crisis team if you have one.

    Samaritans – call 116 123, www.samaritans.org/how-we-can-help/contact-samaritan/, email jo@samaritans.org

    Campaign Against Living Miserably (CALM) – call 0800 58 5858 5pm to midnight every day, live chat and WhatsApp also available 5pm to midnight through: www.thecalmzone.net/suicide-prevention-helpline

    Papyrus – prevention of young suicide HOPELINE247 call 0800 068 4141 text 88247 website www.papyrus-uk.org/ email pat@papyrus-uk.org

76. Divall, R. (2017) "Hope and its Therapeutic Potential", *accord.* Winter, pp. 19-22.

77. Adapted from *THE LIFE CYCLE COMPLETED: A Review* by Erik H. Erikson. Copyright © 1982 by Rikan Enterprises, Ltd. Used by permission of W.W. Norton & Company, Inc.

78. Benner, D. (2012) *Spirituality and the Awakening Self.* Grand Rapids: Brazos Press, pp. 41.

79. Kandiah, K. (2014) *Paradoxology.* London: Hodder & Stoughton.

80. Martinez-Marti, L., Avia, M. & Hernandez-Lloreda, (2018) "Effects of an appreciation of beauty randomized controlled trial web-based intervention on appreciation of beauty and well-being", *Psychology of Aesthetics Creativity and the Arts.* 12(3), pp.272-283.

81. Lama, D., Tutu, D., Abrams, D. (2016) *The Book of Joy.* London: Hutchinson, pp. 347-248.

82. Sacks, J. (2012) *The Great Partnership: God, Science and the Search for Meaning.* London: Hodder & Stoughton Ltd, pp. 288.

The Association of Christians in Counselling and Linked Professions (ACC) is a Christian professional membership body for those involved in counselling and psychotherapy, as well as linked professions, that is: pastoral care, coaching and mentoring, and spiritual direction.

Our website www.acc-uk.org is a place for members of the public to find qualified, ethical professionals who are also Christian. As further assurance our counsellors and psychotherapists are on ACC's accredited register under the UK's Professional Standards Authority. Importantly, ACC members work with people of all faiths and none.

Our members are from various Christian denominations and traditions, united by the same faith, professions and callings. We are an established professional voice that promotes the therapeutic importance of considering a person's spirituality and religious faith as being intrinsic to their psychological wellbeing, and a person's psychological wellbeing being similarly intrinsic to the health of their spiritual and religious life.

Also available

ISBN: 978-1-912863-29-7

To order scan the code below

In this brave book Sarah Grace puts her life on the line in every sense. Woven throughout the book is the story of her life's journey and its vicissitudes. Ultimately it is a tale of optimism, faith and of light coming out of darkness. The moving accounts of those she has met along the way, will inspire others to keep going through their bleakest times. Spiritual and emotionally engaging it bears witness to the ways in which hope and meaning may emerge where least expected.

Joy Schaverien PhD, Jungian psychoanalyst, author of Boarding School Syndrome